START READING

Other titles in this series

ADAMS & LLANAS
Go on Reading

ADAMS & LLANAS
Extend your Reading

LEBAUER
Reading Skills for the Future

MOLLER & WHITESON
Cloze in Class

START READING

Reading Resources in International English

1

Leslie Adams and Angela Llanas
Anglo-Mexican Institute, Mexico City

PERGAMON PRESS

OXFORD · NEW YORK · TORONTO · SYDNEY · PARIS · FRANKFURT

U.K.	Pergamon Press Ltd., Headington Hill Hall, Oxford OX3 0BW, England
U.S.A.	Pergamon Press Inc., Maxwell House, Fairview Park, Elmsford, New York 10523, U.S.A.
CANADA	Pergamon Press Canada Ltd., Suite 104, 150 Consumers Road, Willowdale, Ontario M2J 1P9, Canada
AUSTRALIA	Pergamon Press (Aust.) Pty Ltd, P.O. Box 544, Potts Point, N.S.W. 2011, Australia
FRANCE	Pergamon Press SARL, 24 Rue des Ecoles, 75240 Paris, Cedex 05, France
FEDERAL REPUBLIC OF GERMANY	Pergamon Press GmbH, Hammerweg 6, D-6242 Kronberg-Taunus, Federal Republic of Germany

First edition 1983

British Library Cataloguing in Publication Data

Adams, Leslie
Start Reading   (Materials for language practice)
1. English language — Text-books for foreigners.
2. Readers — 1950-
I. Title   II. Llanas, Angela
III. Series
428.4'076   PE1128
ISBN 0-08-029435-9

Printed in Great Britain by A. Wheaton & Co. Ltd., Exeter

ACKNOWLEDGEMENTS

The Publisher gratefully acknowledges the following sources of visual materials used in the compilation of this book:

Boulton Hawker Films Ltd., Canadian Government Tourist Office, Los Folkloristas, The Mansell Collection, Ronald Sheridan, John Topham, United States Tourist Service, Worcester Art Museum.

CONTENTS

UNIT 1

TEXT 1

This is London. London is the capital of England.

This is Elizabeth II. She is the Queen of England, Northern Ireland, Scotland and Wales. She is also the Queen of certain Commonwealth countries (e.g. Canada, Australia and New Zealand).

This is Buckingham Palace. Queen Elizabeth and her family live in Buckingham Palace.

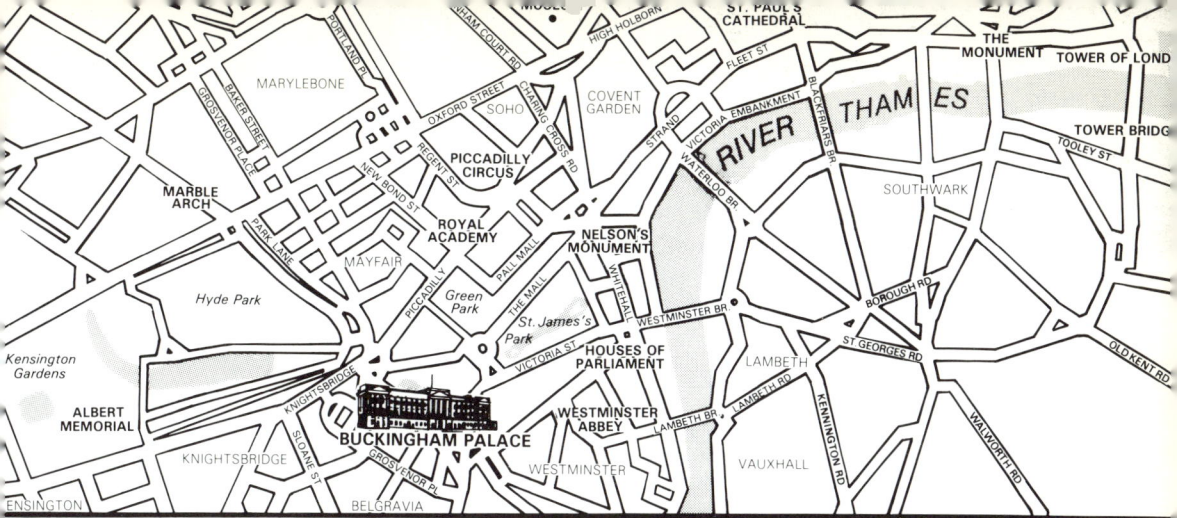

This is a map of London. London is a very big and a very beautiful city. Buckingham Palace is in The Mall.

The Queen leaves Buckingham Palace in the summer and goes to Scotland.

This is Prince Charles and that is his wife, Diana, Princess of Wales. He is Queen Elizabeth's son.

This is Balmoral Castle. Balmoral Castle is the Queen's home in Scotland.

9

A. *Are the following statements true of false? Circle **T** for true or **F** for false.*

1 London is the capital of England.	T	F
2 Elizabeth II is Queen of India.	T	F
3 Buckingham Palace is the Queen's house in Scotland	T	F
4 The Mall is a street in London.	T	F
5 Diana is Charles's sister.	T	F

B. *Make correct sentences out of the following words.*

1 Queen   Elizabeth   of   Ireland   Northern   Queen   the   is.
2 Queen and family Elizabeth her in Buckingham live Palace.
3 very   big   city   and   beautiful   very   a   London   is.
4 The   Queen   to   Scotland   the   in   summer   goes.
5 home   Scotland   the   Queen's   in   Castle   Balmoral   is.

TEXT 2

A. *This is some information about Canada. Study it.*

Canada — very big (second largest country in the world) — very beautiful.
Capital — Ottawa
Queen — Elizabeth II
Queen's representative in Canada — Governor General
Governor General's official residence — Rideau Hall.

B. *Now look at the following pictures and fill in the missing words.*

This . . . . Canada.

Canada is a . . . .

and a . . . . country.

This . . . .

She . . . . Queen of Canada.

. . . . Ottawa. The Queen's . . . .

Ottawa is . . . . in . . . . is

. . . . the Governor General. The Governor

. . . . General . . . . in Rideau Hall.

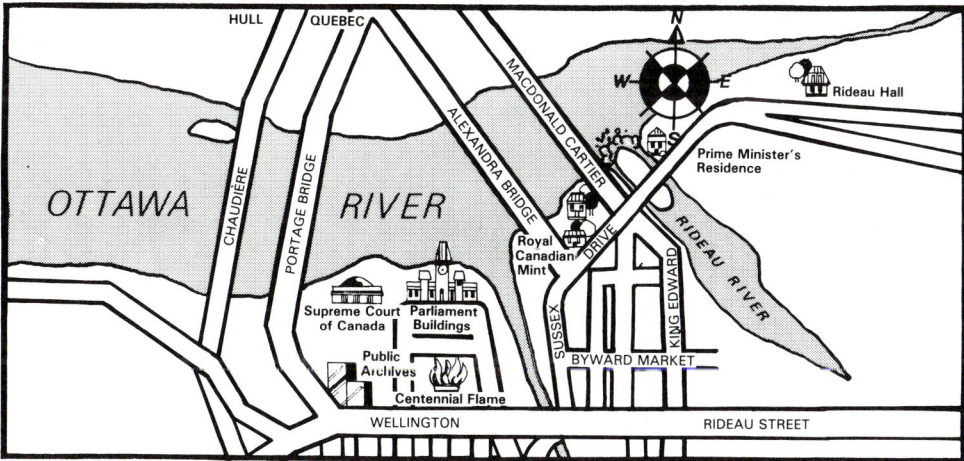

This is . . . .

of Ottawa. Rideau Hall . . . .

. . . . the

north-east of Ottawa.

Oral Reinforcement

This is Marco Antonio Sánchez Diaz. Marco Antonio wants to go to Edinburgh. Edinburgh is the capital of Scotland. He would like to visit all the places of interest.

This is a map of Edinburgh. Indicate to Marco the places of interest.

Example: That is St. Giles's Cathedral. St. Giles's Cathedral is in . . . .

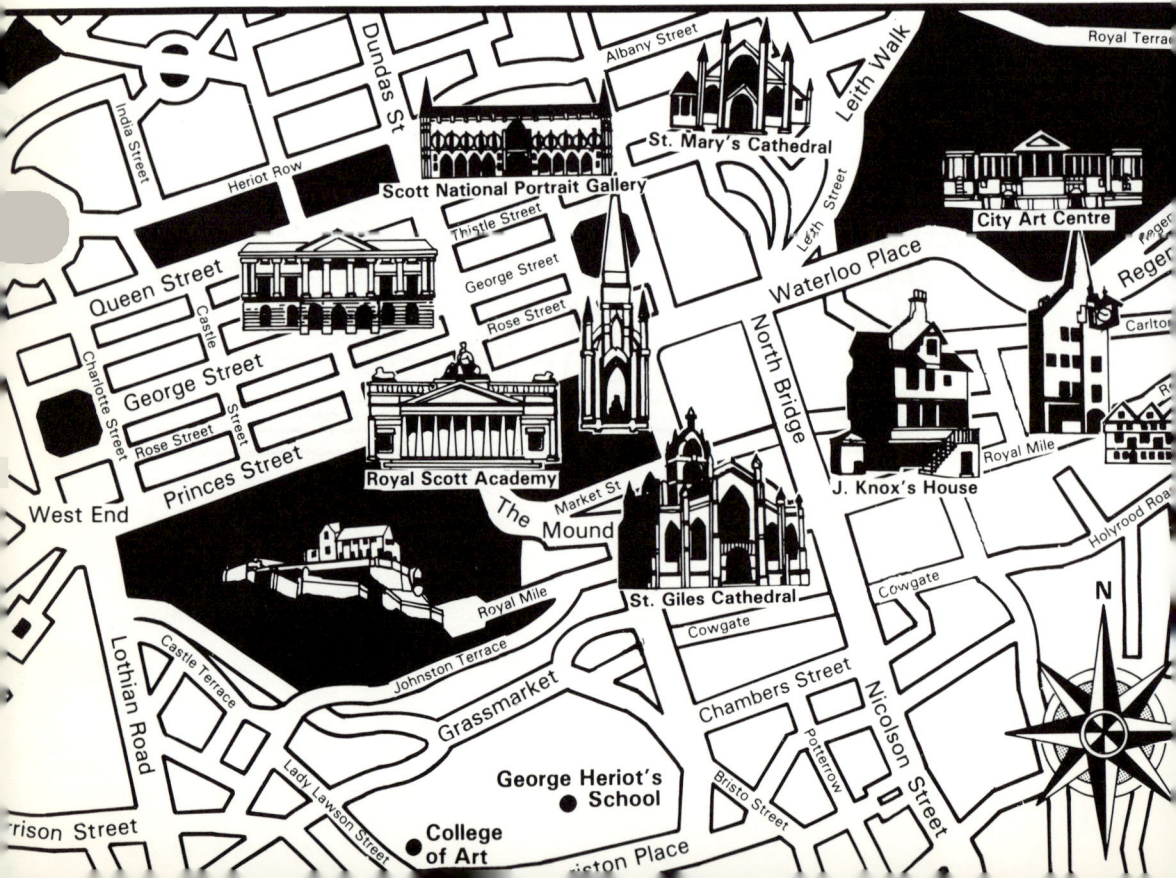

TEXT 3

This beautiful bird is an osprey. Ospreys live on all the continents, except Antarctica. In Great Britain, ospreys live in Scotland.

Ospreys eat fish. They catch the fish in their talons.

Ospreys make their nests at the top of pines and spruces. They come back to the same nest year after year. Ospreys normally lay three eggs. Incubation takes thirty-five days. The female osprey stays with the young. The male feeds the family three to five fish per day.

14

A. *Underline the correct statement.*

1 There are ospreys in Antarctica.
  There are no ospreys in Antarctica.

2 Ospreys live all over Great Britain.
  Ospreys live in only one part of Great Britain.

3 Ospreys live on fish.
  Ospreys live on small land animals.

4 An osprey makes its nest on the top of a cliff.
  Ospreys use the same nest for many years.

6 A female osprey usually lays three eggs.
  A female osprey sometimes lays three eggs but normally lays more.

7 The osprey chicks hatch in five weeks.
  The osprey chicks hatch in six weeks.

8 Both the parent birds stay in the nest with the chicks.
  The female bird stays in the nest with the chicks.

9 The male bird normally catches fish for the family.
  The female bird normally catches fish for the family.

10 A family of ospreys eats more than five fish a day.
   A family of ospreys eats up to five fish a day.

B. *Fill in the missing words.*

There are no ospreys . . . . England, but there are . . . . in Scotland.

They make . . . . nests at the top . . . . coniferous trees. Ospreys

come . . . . to the same nest . . . . many years. Incubation of

. . . . eggs takes thirty-five . . . . The female ospreys stays

. . . . the chicks in the . . . . and the male osprey . . . . three

to five fish . . . . day for his family.

Before reading Text I, read the following questions. Then try to find the answers in the text.

1 What is Arizona like?
2 What does Janie want to do in the future?
3 Would she like to work in Los Angeles?

TEXT 1

This is Janie Davis. She is a young American girl. She lives with her family in Arizona.

Arizona is in the south-western part of the United States.

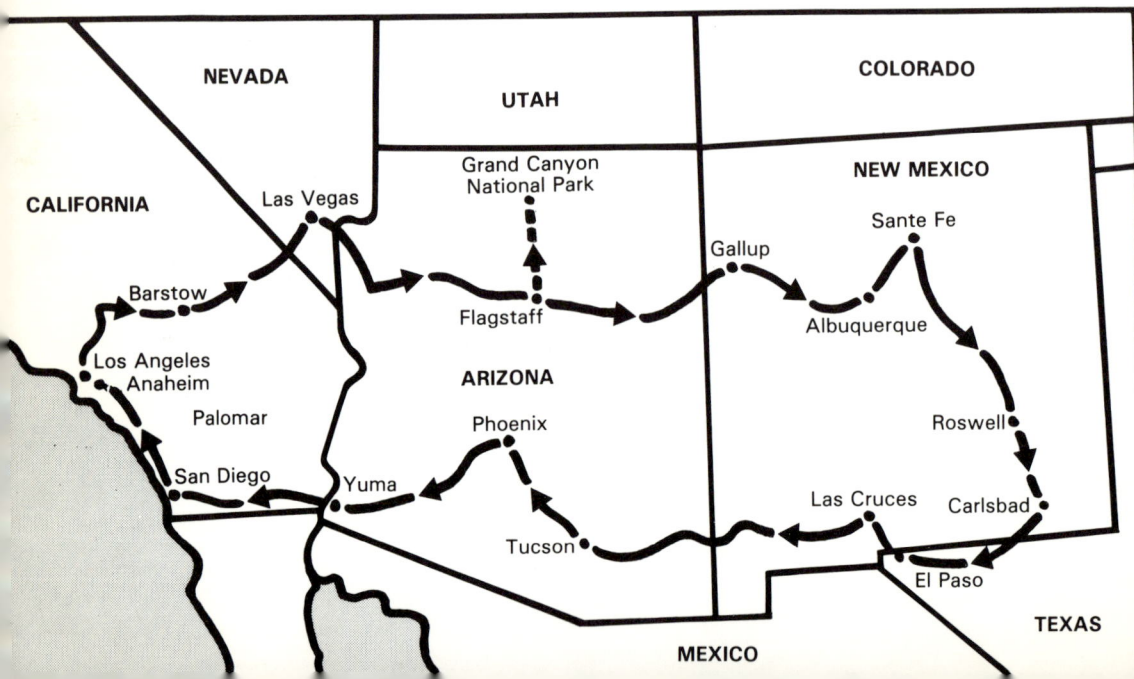

It is a dry and mountainous part of the country.

Janie lives in Phoenix. At the moment, she is a student at Scottsdale High School. This is in the rich part of town. She lives on 10th Avenue with her mother and father and her younger brother and sister.

Her brother is in Junior High School, and ner sister is still at primary school.

After high school, Janie wants to go to Tucson. She wants to study primary teaching at the University of Arizona in Tucson. Some day in the future, Janie would like to teach poor children in one of the big cities in the United States — New York, Chicago or Los Angeles.

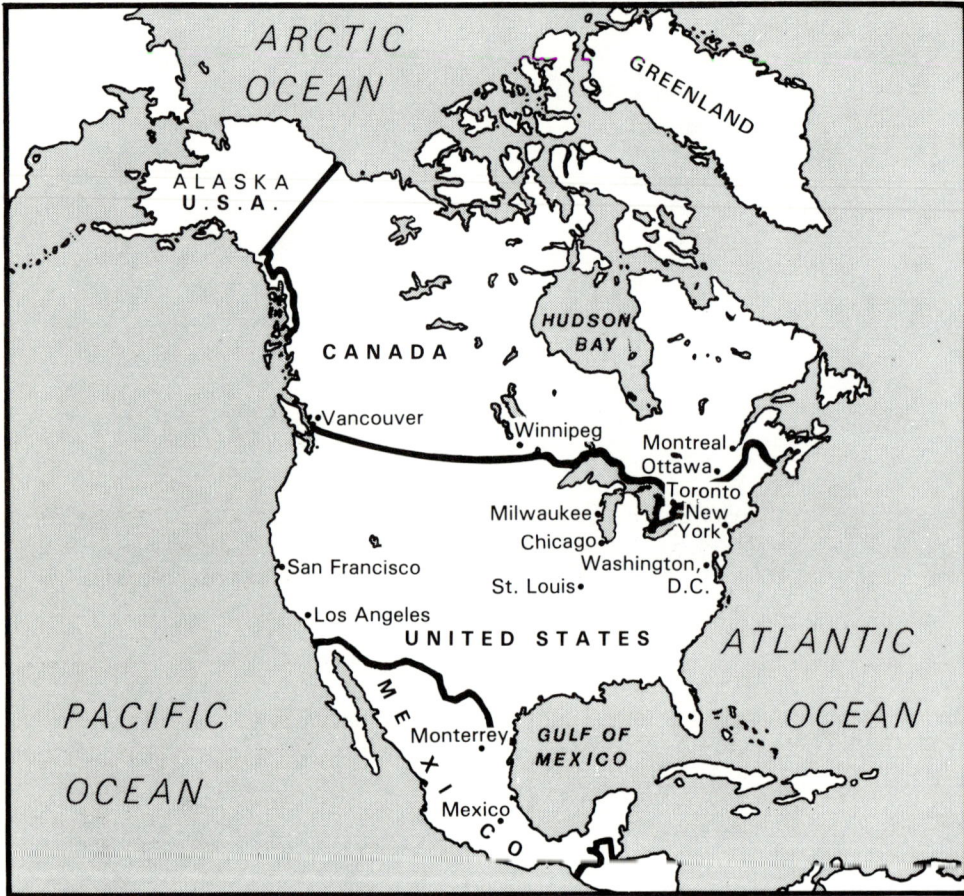

A. *Choose the best answer, and indicate your reason for choosing it.*

1 Janie is
(a) poor
(b) probably rich
(c) old
(d) rich

2 Janie lives
(a) in the North-West
(b) in Arizona
(c) in the South-West
(d) in two of the above

3 Arizona is
   (a) humid
   (b) flat
   (c) dry
   (d) windy

4 The University of Arizona is in
   (a) Phoenix
   (b) Los Angeles
   (d) Tucson
   (d) Scottsdale

5 Janie would like to
   (a) teach rich children
   (b) teach poor children in Tucson
   (c) teach rich children in a big city
   (d) teach poor children in Los Angeles, Chicago or New York.

TEXT 2

There are many deserts in the world; some famous ones are the Sahara Desert in Africa, the Gobi Desert in Mongolia and the Sonora Desert in Arizona and northern Mexico. There is only a little water in the desert, but several plants do grow there. Here are two of these plants.

This is the Century Plant. It grows in the American deserts. This plant lives for many years. At the end of its life, this stalk grows about five meters into the air. Beautiful flowers grow from the stalk. Then the plant dies.

This is the Organ Pipe Cactus. It grows in the desert areas of southern, central and northern America. This plant stores water in its thick stems. It has very sharp spines. These spines protect the plant from animals.

Also, there are many animals adapted to life in the desert. The Gila Monster is one of them.

This is the Gila Monster. There are only two poisonous lizards in the world. The Gila Monster is one of them. It lives on small birds, eggs and young mammals. It stores this food in its long tail. Sometimes it bites human beings. Its bite is very dangerous.

A. *Are the following statements true or false? Circle **T** for true and **F** for false.*

1	There are not many deserts in the world.	T	F
2	There are plants in the desert.	T	F
3	The Century Plant grows in the Sahara Desert.	T	F
4	The Century Plant has beautiful flowers many years before it dies.	T	F
5	The Organ Pipe Cactus grows in the deserts of the American Continent.	T	F

B. *The following statements are false. Make them true.*

1 The Organ Pipe Cactus stores water in the flowers.

No! The Organ Pipe Cactus . . . .

2 Its sharp spines protect the Organ Pipe Cactus from man.

. . . .

3 There are no animals properly adapted to life in the desert.

. . . .

4 No lizard in the world today is poisonous.

. . . .

5 The Gila Monster is not a poisonous lizard.

. . . .

C. *Here are some photographs taken on the sea-shore. Study them and fill in the missing words.*

Several plants . . . . in the sea

and appear on the sea-shore. Here

. . . . two of . . . .

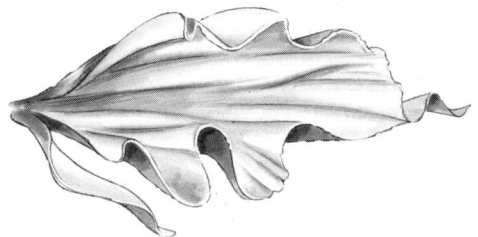

. . . . is a seaweed. It appears . . . . muddy sea-shores.

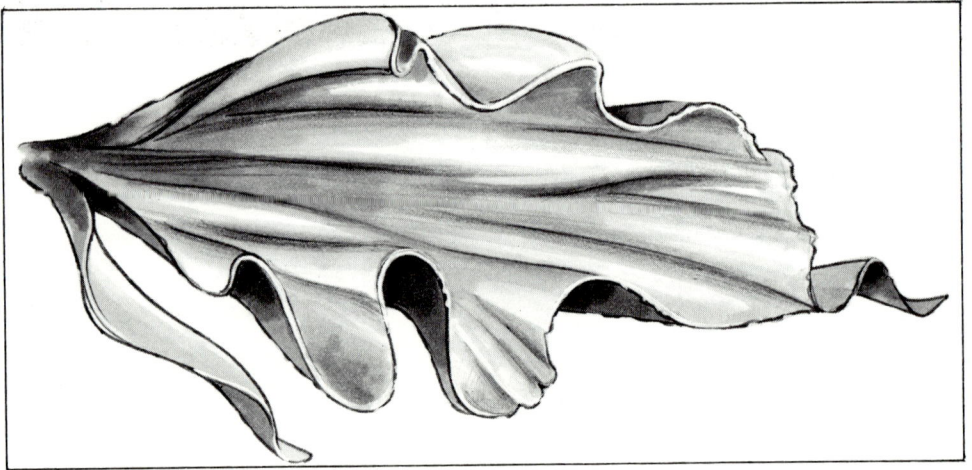

. . . . a seaweed. It . . . . off the north-eastern coast of Australia,

among other places. It helps to build coral reefs — the Great Barrier Reef, for

example.

Also . . . . are many animals . . . . to life in the sea.

Oral Reinforcement

This is a photo of a sea urchin. Study the information and make statements about this animal.

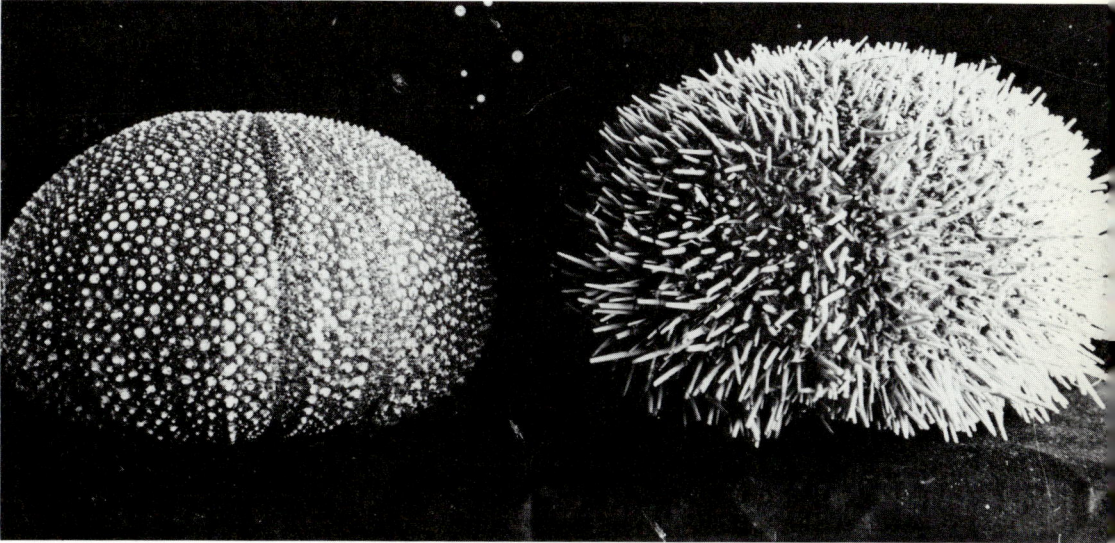

round
covered with spines
tube-feet between spines

eat . . . . seaweed

people eat . . . . some varieties

of . . . .

TEXT 1

1 This interview appeared last week in a newspaper for the English-speaking
2 community in Mexico City. The reporter was speaking to Adrian Nieto, who is a
3 member of the group 'Los Folkloristas'. 'Los Folkloristas' is a famous folk
4 music group in Mexico.

5 *Interviewer:* How many musicians are there in 'Los Folkloristas', Adrian?
6 *Nieto:* There are seven. Five men and two women.
7 *Interviewer:* And how many instruments does the group play?
8 *Neito:* Well I don't know, precisely. Between fifty and sixty.
9 *Interviewer:* Oh, I see.
10 *Nieto:* Yes, we play wind, string and percussion instruments.
11 *Interviewer:* Is 'Los Folkloristas' a group that only plays instruments?
12 *Nieto:* No, of course not. We sing as well.
13 *Interviewer:* Does the group have any records on the market?
14 *Nieto:* Yes, ten. In fact, we have our own record company. It's called
15 'Discos Pueblo'.
16 *Interviewer:* Do you play only in Mexico?
17 *Nieto:* Well, we play in Mexico a lot, of course, but we also play in the
18 United States, Cuba, Costa Rica, Colombia, Italy and East
19 Germany, from time to time.
20 *Interviewer* Good gracious! Which other countries would you like to visit?
21 *Nieto:* I would like to go to the U.S.S.R. and China.
22 *Interviewer:* That would be interesting. And what are your immediate plans for
23 the future?
24 *Nieto:* I would like to know even more about the history of Latin American
25 music and especially the history of Mexican music.
26 *Interviewer:* Thank you very much Adrian. It's been a pleasure talking to you.

A. *Write **YES** or **NO** as appropriate in the space provided.*

1 This interview appeared on television. . . . .

2 Adrian Nieto is a member of a famous folk group. . . . .

3 There are five women and two men in the group. . . . .

4 'Los Folkloristas' play only in Mexico. . . . .

5 Adrian Nieto would like to go to the U.S.S.R. and China. . . . .

B. *Answer the following Questions.*

1 How many musicians are there in 'Los Folkloristas'?

. . . .

2 How many instruments does the group play?

. . . .

3 Does the group have any records on the market?

. . . .

4 Which countries does the group play in from time to time?

. . . .

5 What are Adrian's immediate plans for the future?

. . . .

C. *Choose the best answer and indicate why you think it is best.*

1 In line 8 'Well, I don't know precisely' refers to
   (a) the group
   (b) the number of musicians
   (c) the number of instruments
   (d) five men and two women

2 In line 9 'Oh, I see' means
   (a) I can see fifty or sixty
   (b) I see five men and two women
   (c) 'Los Folkloristas'
   (d) I understand

3 In line 12 '. . . as well' means
   (a) as much
   (b) in addition
   (c) a lot
   (d) very well

4 In line 19 '. . . from time to time' means
   (a) sometimes
   (b) often
   (c) very often
   (d) frequently

5 In line 24 '. . . even more' means
   (a) more often
   (b) more frequently
   (c) a larger amount
   (d) equal quantity

TEXT 2

Athens is the capital of Greece.

Tourists visit Greece because they want to see the Acropolis. This is a photograph of the Parthenon. It is one of the seven wonders of the Ancient World.

In this photograph, you can see how the Parthenon dominates the Acropolis.

Of course, in Greece they speak Greek, but many Greeks (waiters, tourist guides, etc.) speak a little English, because tourism is Greece's most important industry. Most tourists like to leave mainland Greece after they visit Athens, Delphi, Corinth, Mycenae and Mount Olympus, to visit some of the beautiful off-shore islands. For instance the island of Mikonos, famous for its romantic white buildings, and the islands of Rhodes and Crete.

One of the most interesting spectacles in Greece is Greek dancing. Traditionally, it is only the men who dance, because the dancers have to be tremendously athletic.

Probably the most famous Greek dishes are *moussaka* and *shishkebabs,* and the best known Greek drinks are *retsina* and *ouzo.*

VASILIS
14A Voukourestiou Street

Menú

Apéritifs and Appetizers

Oúzo	121 dr.
Mastíka	90 dr.
Retsina	103 dr.
Mezé (cheese, tomato, cucumber and olives)	172 dr.
Dzadzíki (cucumber with yoghourt and garlic)	108 dr.
Tyrópitta (cheese pie)	134 dr.
Psarósoupa (fish broth with vegetables)	90 dr.
Avgolémono (chicken broth with rice and eggs)	95 dr.

Main Courses

Souzoukákia (meatballs and rice, in egg and lemon sauce)	386 dr.
Moussaká (mincemeat and aubergine pie)	407 dr.
Dolmádes (cabbage leaves with mince and rice stuffing)	342 dr.
Shishkebabs (grilled meat on a skewer)	237 dr.
Kotópoulo (chicken stuffed with rice and cheese)	420 dr.
Garídes (prawns in lemon)	291 dr.

Vegetables

Visélia (peas)	60 dr.
Fasólia Fréska (french beans)	75 dr.
Prókola (broccoli)	71 dr.
Kilokíthia (small pumpkins)	80 dr.
Melintzánes (egg plants)	66 dr.
Agináres (artichokes)	79 dr.

Desserts

Yaoúrti (yoghourt)	40 dr.
Baklavá (flaky pastry with custard filling)	114 dr.
Fráoules (strawberries)	106 dr.
Yarmádes (yellow peaches)	89 dr.

N.B. Did you notice that there are Century Plants in Greece too? This is due to the arid climate.

A. *The following statements are false. Make them true.*

1 Corinth is the capital of Greece.

No. . . . .

2 The Parthenon is a famous modern building.

. . . .

3 There are not many visitors to Greece.

. . . .

4 Tourists only like to visit mainland Greece.

. . . .

5 Traditionally, it is only the women who dance in Greece.

. . . .

B. *Match the phrases in column **A** with those in column **B** to make correct sentences.*

	A	B
1	Athens is popular	is part of the Acropolis.
2	The Parthenon	like to visit the off-shore islands.
3	Many people in Greece	because people want to see the Acropolis.
4	Tourists in Greece	are moussaka and shishkebabs.
5	Popular Greek dishes	can speak a little English.

1 . . . .

2 . . . .

3 . . . .

4 . . . .

5 . . . .

TEXT 3

This is the timetable of a seven-day cruise of the Greek islands and nearby Turkey. The port of departure is Piraeus, which is the port of Athens. Study the timetable carefully.

DAY	PORT	ARRIVAL	DEPARTURE
FRIDAY	Piraeus	—	18:30
SATURDAY	Santorini	06:30	10:15
	Knossos	15:30	19:00
SUNDAY	Rhodes	07:00	20:30
MONDAY	Ephesus	07:00	12:00
TUESDAY	Istanbul	14:30	—
WEDNESDAY	Istanbul	—	12:00
THURSDAY	Delos	10:30	12:30
	Mikonos	14:30	23:00
FRIDAY	Piraeus	07:00	—

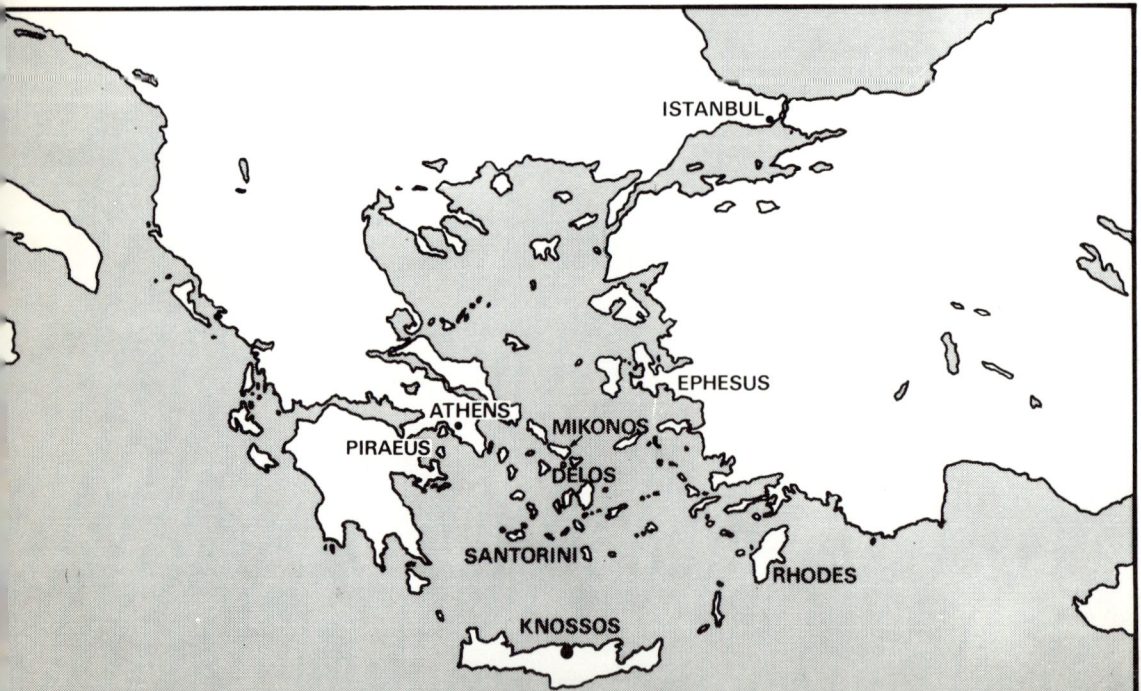

A. *Are the following statements true or false? Circle **T** for true or **F** for false.*

1 The tourists arrive at Knossos on Saturday afternoon.   T   F
2 Tourists on this cruise stay in Istanbul for one day.   T   F
3 The tour goes from Istanbul to Mikonos.   T   F
4 The tourists on this cruise stay in Delos for a long time.   T   F
5 The tourists on this tour visit two places in Turkey.   T   F

Oral Reinforcement

Make statements about the cruise.
e.g. On Friday, the ship leaves Piraeus at half-past six.

TEXT 1

Sydney, Australia,
October 3rd, 19—

Dear Hazel,

1 It's very nice out here — not at all
2 what I had expected. The people in Australia
3 are very friendly in general. I like my
4 new boss, too. In fact, I like all the people at
5 the office. The weather is much nicer than
6 in England. Imagine!
7 I have air-conditioning at home.
8 Oh, one of the people at the office got me a
9 really comfortable flat. It overlooks the
10 harbour, which is nice.
11 Listen, Hazel! There's only one
12 problem. I miss you! I really do! Won't
13 you reconsider your decision? I'm twenty-
14 eight, you know. It's time I was married!
15 You say you're too young to marry me,
16 but I don't agree. It's your mother who
17 doesn't care for me — that's obvious! But
18 you're twenty-two now, you know. You
19 must make your own decisions.
20 Hazel, we like the same things. I like
21 films and so do you. You like dancing and
22 so do I. Give it a try, Hazel! Come out here
23 for Christmas. Stay a few months! I think
24 my boss will give you a job. We can start
25 a new life out here together in Australia.
26 Think about it carefully and write to me
soon. All my love. Willy.

Look for the answers to these questions in the text.

1 Are Willy and Hazel in the same country?
2 Do they know each other well?
3 What does Willy want Hazel to do?

34

A. *Write the answers to the following questions.*

1 Where does Willy live?

. . . .

2 What is Willy's flat like?

. . . .

3 What things do Hazel and Willy both like?

. . . .

4 What does Willy want Hazel to do this Christmas?

. . . .

5 What can Hazel and Willy start in Australia?

. . . .

What do the following words and phrases refer to?

1 'out here' in line 1

    (a) England.
    (b) the garden.
    (c) Australia.
    (d) Sydney Harbour.

2 'at home' in line 6

    (a) the comfortable flat in Australia.
    (b) the comfortable flat in England.
    (c) the office.
    (d) Australia in general.

3 'who doesn't care for me' in line 16 means

    (a) I don't like her.
    (b) she doesn't like you.
    (c) you don't like me.
    (d) she doesn't like me.

4 'Give it a try' in line 21 refers to

    (a) life with Willy.
    (b) life with Willy in Australia.
    (c) life with her mother.
    (d) work in an Australian office.

5 'So do I' in line 21 means.

    (a) I don't agree.
    (b) but I don't think so.
    (c) and I also like that.
    (d) but I don't like that.

TEXT 2

Approximately 1.2 per cent of the population in Australia is Aboriginal. About half the Aboriginal people nowadays live in towns and cities, and these people participate at various levels in the life of the Australian community. However, there are still many Aborigines who live a tribally-oriented life in the remoter parts of the Australian continent.

There is no legal discrimination against the Aborigines, but in reality they do not have the same educational or employment possibilities as other Australians.

The Australian Government has a department of Aboriginal Affairs. This department recognizes the right of the Aborigines to own their traditional lands. Since 1976, the Aborigines have owned land in the Northern Territory. No other state in Australia provides land rights for the Aborigines.

The Aborigines are rich in culture. Aboriginal tribes have their own religion, their own laws, their own social organization, ceremonies and mythology. Aboriginal paintings, engravings and dances are very beautiful. Now, in some communities, Aboriginal children are being educated in their own language.

A. *Choose the best answer and indicate your reason for choosing it.*

1 In Australia
    (a) a large percentage of the population is Aboriginal.
    (b) most of the people are Aboriginal.
    (c) a small percentage of the population is Aboriginal.

2 The Aboriginal people
   (a) live in the towns and cities of Australia.
   (b) live only in the remoter parts of the Australian continent.
   (c) live in the towns and cities and the remoter parts of the Australian continent.

3 In reality
   (a) there is discrimination against the Aboriginal people.
   (b) there is no discrimination against any group of people in Australia.
   (c) the Aboriginal people have the same educational and employment possibilities as white Australians.

4 The Aboriginal people
   (a) have no land rights.
   (b) own some of their traditional lands in the Northern Territory.
   (c) own their traditional lands in all the states of Australia.

5 The Aborigines are rich in culture
   (a) but their paintings, engravings and dances are not very attractive.
   (b) but now cannot speak their native language.
   (c) but are economically and educationally discriminated against.

B. *Put the following sequences of words in the correct order to make sentences.*

1 in / Aborigines / cities / the / remote / live / and / areas.

. . . .

2 has / Goverment / for / some / Aborigines / the / services.

. . . .

3 the / Territory / in / some / Aborigines / land / Northern / own.

. . . .

4 culture / the / have / their / own / Aborigines.

. . . .

5 own / can / study / language / Aboriginal / their / in / children

. . . .

This is a photograph of Dame Joan Sutherland. She is a famous opera singer. Joan Sutherland comes from Australia.

Below is some information about Dame Joan Sutherland's life. Study it.

Dame Joan Sutherland

Date of birth	—	7 November 1926.
Place of origin	—	Sydney, New South Wales
1947	—	Made her debut as Dido in Purcell's *Dido and Aeneas*.
1952	—	Joined the famous Royal Opera Company at Convent Garden in London. Many famous parts, including the Countess in *Figaro,* Desdemona in *Othello,* Lucia in *Lucia di Lammermoor,* etc., etc.
1954	—	Married Richard Bonynge.
1959	—	Sang with the Vienna State Opera.
1960	—	Debut in France.
1961 – 62	—	Sang with the Metropolitan Opera Company in New York.
1962 – 63	—	Appeared at the famous opera house called La Scala in Milan.

Dame Joan Sutherland has made many records in Great Britain and France.

A. *Taking your information from Text 3, plot Dame Joan Sutherland's professional progress throughout the world on this map.*

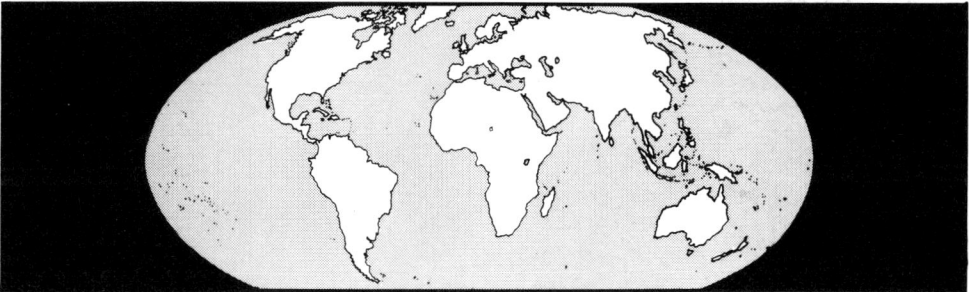

B. *Now write a short biography of Dame Joan Sutherland. It has been started for you.*

Dame Joan Sutherland was born on 7 November 1926 in . . . .

. . . .

. . . .

. . . .

. . . .

. . . .

TEXT 1

These pictures indicate what a passenger in a DC – 10 jet should do in case of an emergency over the sea.

1

. . . .

. . . .

2

. . . .

. . . .

3

. . . .

. . . .

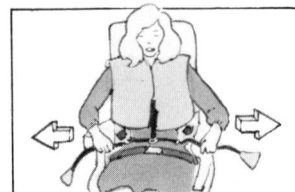

4

. . . .

. . . .

5

. . . .

. . . .

6

. . . .

. . . .

. . . .

A. *The following instructions describe what you can see in the pictures. Copy the appropriate instruction beside each picture.*

If the life-jacket does not inflate blow into the tubes.

Pass the strings round your waist.

Pass the ends of the strings through the loops.

When you leave the aeroplane inflate the life-jacket by pulling the strings with the red tabs smartly downwards.

Pull the strings firmly into position.

Put the life-jacket over your head.

B. *Look at the pictures in Text 1 and the instructions you have written in.*

Below is the text an air hostess might use when giving the obligatory emergency instructions on a transatlantic flight. Some of the words she might say are missing. Fill them in.

In the unlikely event . . . . the aeroplane landing on . . . . water put your

life-jacket, ... is located under your . . . . over your head. Pass

. . . . strings round your waist . . . . through the loops. Pull

. . . . strings firmly into position . . . . this. There are several

. . . . exits on this aircraft. . . . . can see the location . . . . the

emergency exits on . . . . picture you will find . . . . the pocket in front

. . . . you. Do not inflate . . . . life-jacket until you leave . . . .

aeroplane. When you do . . . . the aeroplane, inflate the . . . . by pulling

the strings . . . . the red tabs smartly . . . . If the life-jacket does

. . . . inflate, blow into these . . . .

41

Before reading Text 2 study the following questions.

1 What is unusual about the 'Breakfast Special'?

2 What jobs do the members of the technical crew have?

3 What items are on the check-list?

4 Who gives the technical crew permission to take off for New York?

5 How fast does Concorde travel?

Now read the text and find the answers to these questions.

TEXT 2

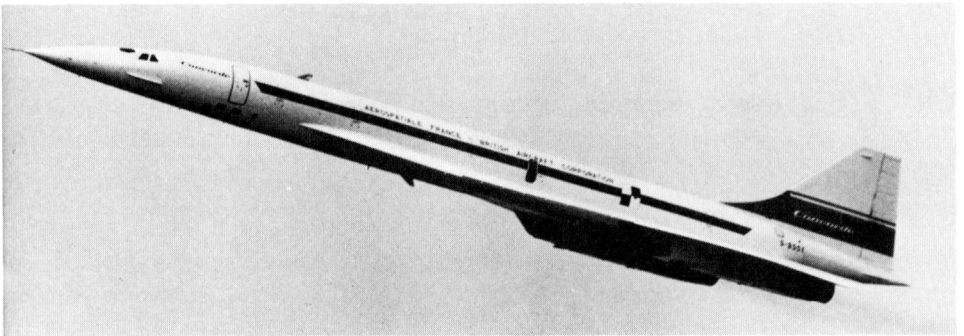

Concorde is the fastest passenger plane in the world. BA 173 is the British Airways 'Breakfast Special'. It leaves Heathrow Airport in London at 9.30 a.m.
   Concorde has a technical crew of three members – the captain, the first officer (co-pilot) and the flight engineer. They go to the briefing-room. There they get all
5 the information required for the flight. The crew check how much fuel they need. This depends on the winds, the temperature and the state of the airports at both ends. Then the crew board Concorde. The check-list is read aloud and everything is carefully checked – the fuel, the flying controls, the hydraulics, electronics, pressurization, oxygen, radio systems, etc.
10   Meanwhile the senior cabin crew officer and his crew members check their areas. Then the passengers come aboard. The cabin crew take them to their seats. Air traffic control gives the technical crew permission to take off for New York. Concorde accelerates fast. She takes off. The crew raise the 'droop snoot' and visor. Concorde climbs across the Atlantic at about 1350 m.p.h. (one
15 mile every 2.7 seconds). She flies 57 000 to 60 000 feet above sea-level.
   The plane reaches New York just three and a half hours after leaving Heathrow at only 8.30 a.m. local time. Concorde beats the sun by one hour! That is what Concorde is all about!

A. *Circle **T** if the following statements are true and **F** if they are false.*

1 Concorde leaves London at 9.30 a.m. and lands in England at
  8.30 a.m.   T   F
2 The cabin crew check the hydraulic system of Concorde before take
  off   T   F
3 The technical crew are responsible for the condition of Concorde
  before take off.   T   F
4 The 'droop snoot' is raised after take off.   T   F
5 The major advantage of Concorde is that it is very comfortable.   T   F

B. *Working in groups, arrange these paragraphs in a logical order.*

Concorde flies across the Atlantic at the supersonic speed of 1350 m.p.h. She climbs to a height of 57000 to 60000 feet above sea-level. The passengers arrive in New York in perfect time to start the working day.

The 'Breakfast Special' takes off from Heathrow Airport at 9.30 a.m. The strange thing is that it arrives in New York at 8.30 a.m. Concorde beats the sun by one hour.

The technical crew arrives at the airport at 8 a.m. and checks that Concorde is in perfect flying condition. The cabin crew check that everything is ready for the passengers.

....

....

....

....

....

....

....

....

....

....

....

Oral Reinforcement

Tell the rest of the class the reasons for your decision.

C. *The following words and phrases appear in Text 2. What do they mean? Choose your answers from (a) (b) (c) or (d).*

1 'crew' in line 3 means
   (a) friends
   (b) group
   (c) team
   (d) organization

2 'state' in line 6 means
   (a) condition
   (b) emotion
   (c) degree
   (d) territory

3 'aloud' in line 7 means
   (a) permitted
   (b) not silently
   (c) accepted
   (d) secretly

4 'meanwhile' in line 10 means
   (a) later
   (b) before
   (c) as a result
   (d) at the same time.

5 'come aboard' in line 11 means
   (a) to go into the airport
   (b) to go to another country
   (c) to go into the aeroplane
   (d) to go into the briefing-room.

TEXT 3

Study this street plan of Mexico City.

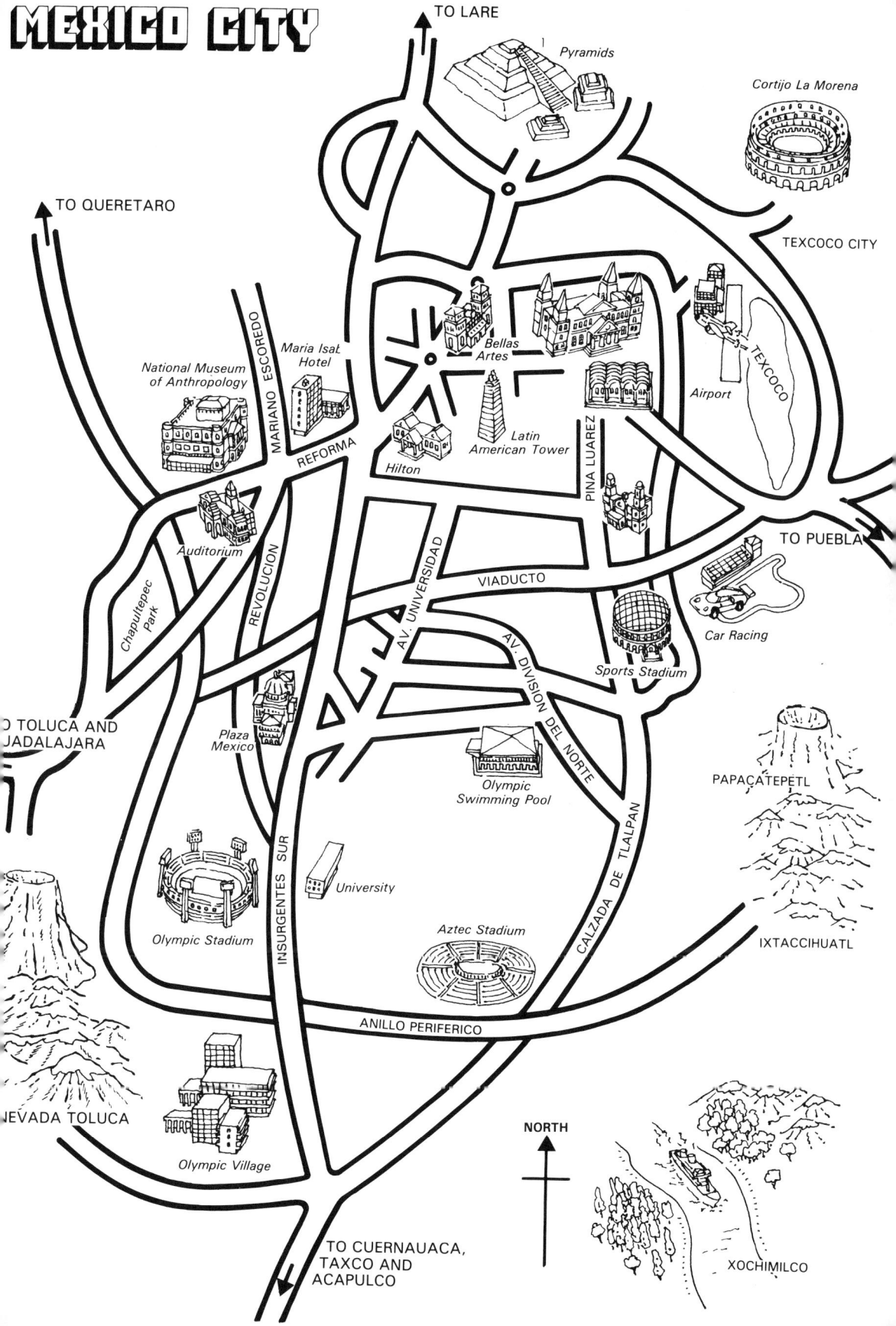

MEXICO CITY

TO LARE

Pyramids

Cortijo La Morena

TO QUERETARO

TEXCOCO CITY

National Museum
of Anthropology

Maria Isab.
Hotel

Bellas
Artes

TEXCOCO

MARIANO ESCOREDO

REFORMA

Latin
American Tower

Airport

Hilton

Auditorium

PINA LUAREZ

TO PUEBLA

Chapultepec
Park

REVOLUCION

VIADUCTO

AV. UNIVERSIDAD

Car Racing

TO TOLUCA AND
GUADALAJARA

AV. DIVISION DEL NORTE

Sports Stadium

Plaza
Mexico

PAPACATEPETL

Olympic
Swimming Pool

CALZADA DE TLALPAN

INSURGENTES SUR

University

Olympic Stadium

Aztec Stadium

IXTACCIHUATL

ANILLO PERIFERICO

NEVADA TOLUCA

Olympic Village

NORTH

TO CUERNAUACA,
TAXCO AND
ACAPULCO

XOCHIMILCO

A. *Write correct statements. Choose your answers from (a) (b) (c) or (d).*

1 The airport is in the . . . . of the city.

(a) north   (c) north-west

(b) south   (d) south-east.

The airport . . . .

2 The Aztec Stadium is located . . . .

(a) on the road to Cuernavaca, Taxco and Acapulco.

(b) near the University of Mexico.

(c) where the Anillo Periferico crosses the Calzada de Tlalpan.

(d) right next to the Olympic swimming-pool.

. . . .

3 There are . . . . to the east of the city.

(a) pyramids   (c) lakes

(b) mountains   (d) sports stadiums

. . . .

4 Viaducto . . . . Insurgentes Sur.

(a) goes over   (c) joins

(b) goes under   (d) runs parrallel to

. . . .

5 A young man staying in the María Isabel Hotel wants to visit the University of Mexico. He can take . . . .

(a) Reforma and Fray Servando.

(b) Reforma and the Anillo Periferico.

(c) Reforma and Avenida Universidad.

(d) Reforma, Revolucion and Insurgentes Sur.

B. Oral Reinforcement

1 Sadie Tomlinson is an American. She is visiting Mexico City for the first time. Sadie is staying at the Hilton Hotel on Reforma. Using the street plan as your guide, indicate to Sadie how she can reach some of the places of interest, e.g.

The Latin American Tower
The Bellas Artes Theatre
The Pyramids
The Zocalo

The Olympic Stadium
Xochimilco
The National Museum of Anthropology
Chapultepec Park, etc.

2 Do you know the alphabet in English? Test each other.
 e.g. How do you spell Chapultepec?
 C – H – A . . ., etc.

White Walls,
Larch Ave.,
Jesmond,
Northumberland,
England.
8th October, 1981.

The Manager,
Château de la Plage,
Palm Beaches Ave.,
Miami,
Florida.

Dear Sir or Madam,

Recently, I visited Miami on a business trip. I stayed in your hotel from 14th to 24th September, 1981. Unfortunately, I feel obliged to make a formal complaint with reference to certain aspects of the service at the Château de la Plage.

In the first place, the Château de la Plage is considered one of the best hotels in Miami. It is also one of the most expensive hotels on Miami Beach. Therefore, I was surprised I could not get a meal in the restaurant when I arrived at 12 p.m. Consider, when it is 12 p.m. in Florida, it is 7 a.m. in England. All I wanted was a simple plate of bacon and eggs! I would like a good hotel to serve international food at all hours.

Secondly, the air-conditioning never functioned correctly during the 10 days of my stay. Every day, I complained about this, but your staff always thought I was exaggerating. But remember, when it is 105°F in Miami, it is only approximately 65°F in England. I am simply not accustomed to such heat.

Finally, my wife, who accompanied me on this trip, caught influenza. We constantly telephoned for the hotel doctor, but he never came. In the end, it was necessary to consult a private doctor, which was very expensive!

I feel I must draw attention to these problems which we encountered in your hotel, for the protection of other foreign visitors.

Yours faithfully

A. *Match the phrases in column* **A** *with those in column* **B** *to make correct sentences.*

A	B
1 Frank Anderson is the man	is one of the most expensive hotels in Miami.
2 The Château de la Plage	does not think the Château de la Plage is a wonderful hotel.
3 Frank Anderson	who stayed in Château de la Plage from 14th to 24th September, 1981.
4 When it is breakfast time in England	to consult a private doctor.
5 In the United States it is very expensive	it is midnight in Florida.

1

. . . .

. . . .

2

. . . .

. . . .

3

. . . .

. . . .

4

. . . .

. . . .

5

. . . .

. . . .

B. *Write the answers to the following questions.*

1 Why did Frank Anderson visit Miami?

....

2 Why does he write to the manager of the Château de la Plage?

....

3 What is the time difference between England and the south-east coast of the United States?

....

4 Why was the fact that the air-conditioning in the Andersons' room at Château de la Plage did not function correctly such a problem for them?

....

5 Why was Mr Anderson anxious to consult the hotel doctor and not a private doctor when his wife caught influenza in Florida?

....

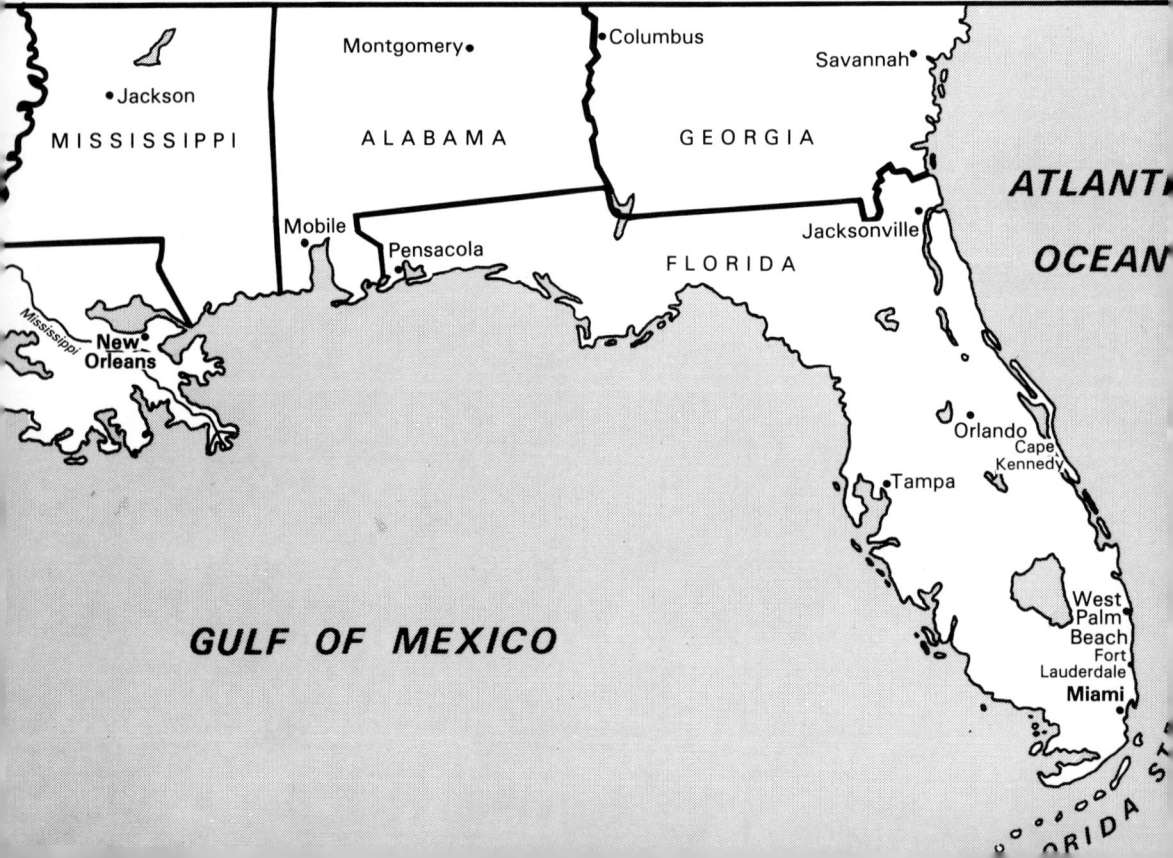

TEXT 2

Study the following questionnaire on the type of holiday you like.

1	Name				
2	Age				
3	Sex	Male	Female		
4	Do you like to spend your holidays		by the sea? ☐ in the country? ☐ resting at home? ☐ in big cities? ☐ travelling from place to place? ☐		
5	What would you like best?		a holiday in your own country. ☐ a holiday abroad. ☐		
6	Do you prefer		to reserve a hotel room in advance? ☐ to camp? ☐ to find accommodation when you arrive? ☐		
7	How do you like to travel?		by plane. ☐ by car. ☐ by train. ☐ by bus. ☐ by ship. ☐		
8	Do you like to spend your holidays		alone? ☐ with your family? ☐ with friends your own age? ☐ with a tour group? ☐		
9	What do you like to do best when you are on holiday?		read books. ☐ meet new people. ☐ swim, ski, hike, etc. ☐ visit ruins. ☐ visit beauty spots. ☐		
10	When you go to a new place, do you prefer		international food? ☐ local dishes? ☐ to take your own food? ☐		

A. *Now fill in the questionnaire by putting a tick (√) in the appropriate boxes. It may be necessary to use more than one tick in some sections.*

Oral Reinforcement

Tell your class about the type of holiday you like.

TEXT 3

How Does A Baby Grow?

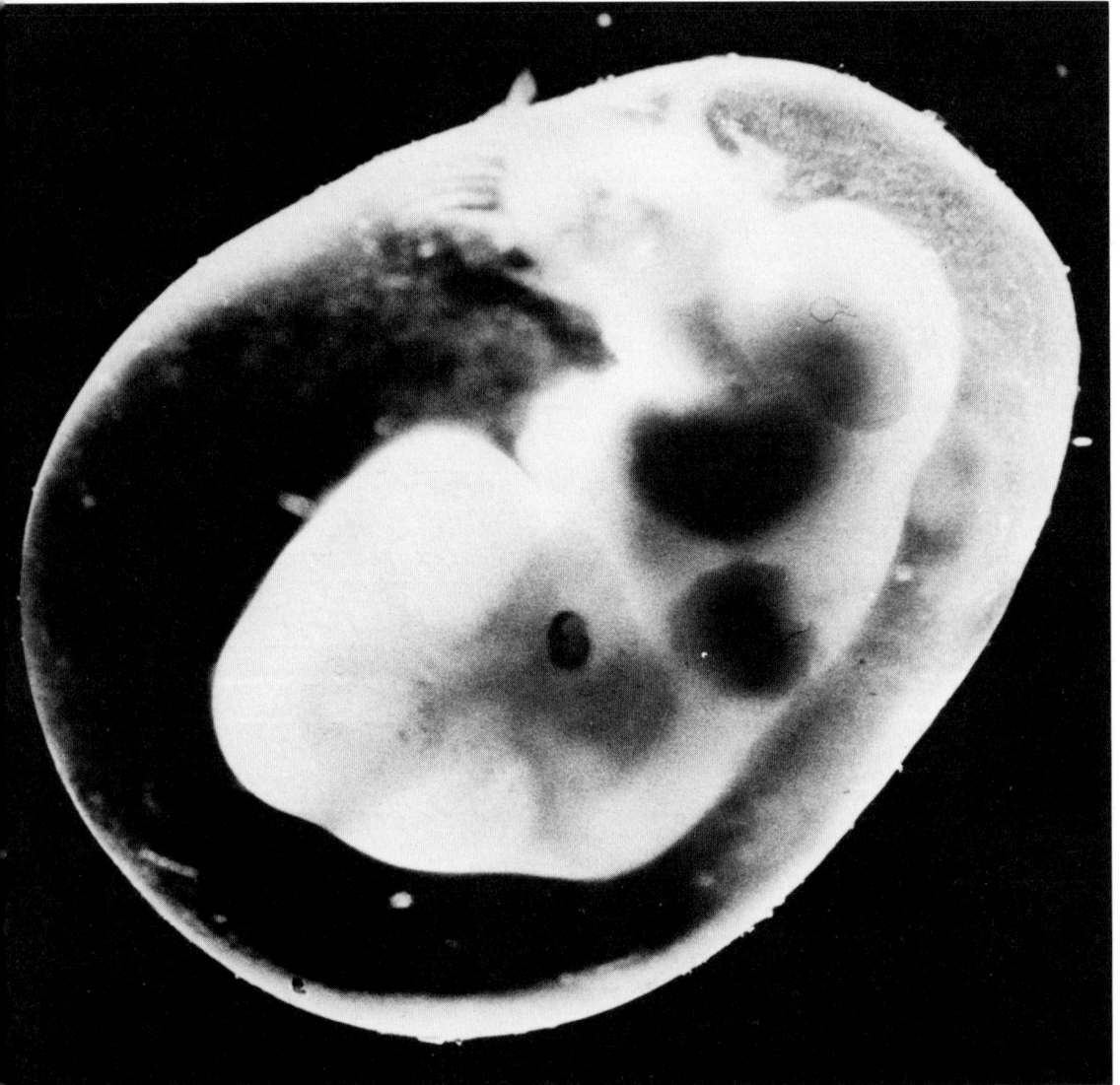

The period of gestation for a human baby is usually two hundred and sixty-six days from the moment of conception. On average, a hundred and six baby boys are born to every hundred baby girls.

The mother usually feels the first movements of her unborn baby between eighteen and twenty weeks from the date of conception. But mothers sometimes do not feel foetal movements until the twenty-fourth week, and this is perfectly normal. In the case of second babies, these movements are usually felt much earlier − at between sixteen and eighteen weeks. The birth of a first baby usually takes twelve hours.

New born babies generally do not eat very much for two or three days. This time is a period of adaptation to life in the outside world. After that, babies usually drink a few ounces of milk every three to four hours round the clock. On average, babies sleep twenty hours a day for the first six weeks of life.

A. *Taking your information from Text 3 fill in the approximate dates for the following events in the development of a baby on the calendar below.*

1 The first movements of the unborn baby (first child).
2 The first movements of the unborn baby (later children).
3 The date of birth.
4 The baby begins to drink every three hours.
5 The baby begins to sleep less than twenty hours a day.

Conception takes place on 1 January.

1982

JANUARY	FEBRUARY	MARCH	APRIL
M T W T F S S	M T W T F S S	M T W T F S S	M T W T F S S
① 2 3	1 2 3 4 5 6 7	1 2 3 4 5 6 7	1 2 3 4
4 5 6 7 8 9 10	8 9 10 11 12 13 14	8 9 10 11 12 13 14	5 6 7 8 9 10 11
11 12 13 14 15 16 17	15 16 17 18 19 20 21	15 16 17 18 19 20 21	12 13 14 15 16 17 18
18 19 20 21 22 23 24	22 23 24 25 26 27 28	22 23 24 25 26 27 28	19 20 21 22 23 24 25
25 26 27 28 29 30 31		29 30 31	26 27 28 29 30
31 DAYS	28 DAYS	31 DAYS	30 DAYS

MAY	JUNE	JULY	AUGUST
M T W T F S S	M T W T F S S	M T W T F S S	M T W T F S S
1 2	1 2 3 4 5 6	1 2 3 4	1
3 4 5 6 7 8 9	7 8 9 10 11 12 13	5 6 7 8 9 10 11	2 3 4 5 6 7 8
10 11 12 13 14 15 16	14 15 16 17 18 19 20	12 13 14 15 16 17 18	9 10 11 12 13 14 15
17 18 19 20 21 22 23	21 22 23 24 25 26 27	19 20 21 22 23 24 25	16 17 18 19 20 21 22
24 25 26 27 28 29 30	28 29 30	26 27 28 29 30	23 24 25 26 27 28 29
31			30 31
31 DAYS	30 DAYS	31 DAYS	31 DAYS

SEPTEMBER	OCTOBER	NOVEMBER	DECEMBER
M T W T F S S	M T W T F S S	M T W T F S S	M T W T F S S
1 2 3 4 5	1 2 3	1 2 3 4 5 6 7	1 2 3 4 5
6 7 8 9 10 11 12	4 5 6 7 8 9 10	8 9 10 11 12 13 14	6 7 8 9 10 11 12
13 14 15 16 17 18 19	11 12 13 14 15 16 17	15 16 17 18 19 20 21	13 14 15 16 17 18 19
20 21 22 23 24 25 26	18 19 20 21 22 23 24	22 23 24 25 26 27 28	20 21 22 23 24 25 26
27 28 29 30	25 26 27 28 29 30 31	29 30	27 28 29 30 31
30 DAYS	31 DAYS	30 DAYS	31 DAYS

B. *Complete the following statements.*

1 The period of gestation is. . . . .
    (a) always the same.
    (b) never the same.
    (c) on average two hundred and sixty-six days from the conception.
    (d) on average two hundred and sixty days after the date of birth.

2 More baby boys . . . .
    (a) are born than baby girls.
    (b) are born bigger than baby girls.
    (c) eat in the first two or three days of life than baby girls.
    (d) sleep twenty hours a day than baby girls.

3 It is perfectly normal . . . .
    (a) for the movements of later babies to be felt by their mothers at thirteen weeks.
    (b) for the movements of first babies to be felt at the twenty-fourth week of pregnancy.
    (c) for mothers never to feel movements from their unborn babies right up until the moment of birth.
    (d) a mother to feel the foetal movements of her first child after fewer weeks of pregnancy than her second child.

4 First children . . . .
    (a) are usually born in less than twelve hours.
    (b) usually take more than twenty-four hours to be born.
    (c) are usually born approximately two hundred days after conception.
    (d) usually take twelve hours to be born.

5 New-born babies
    (a) do not sleep very much.
    (b) eat a lot.
    (c) sleep the whole day.
    (d) do not eat much for the first two or three days of life.

C. *The words in Column I all appear in the text. Find them and read the sentences they appear in, then match them with the words that mean the same in Column 2.*

1	2
period	completely
sometimes	subsequent
perfectly	occasionally
later	length of time.

....

....

....

....

....

....

....

....

....

....

....

....

....

....

....

....

UNIT 7

TEXT 1

Here are some menus from different types of restaurants. Study them.

A

TODAY'S SELECTIONS

SOUPS:
- Cream of mushroom
- Tomato
- Mixed vegetable

MAIN COURSE:
- Spaghetti with meatballs
- Chicken and French fries
- Veal cutlet with mashed potatoes
(green vegetables included
with all meat dishes)

DESSERTS:
- Ice cream (chocolate, strawberry
or vanilla)
- Peaches and cream
- Fruit pie (apple or apricot)

Tea or Coffee

B

Dinners

No. 1
- China Town soup
- Pork, chicken or shrimp chow mein
- White rice
- Soy sauce, mustard Jasmine tea
- Almond cookies

* With 2 orders add 1 free egg roll

No. 2
- Shark's fin and chicken soup with oyster sauce
- White rice. Soy sauce
- Six fried shrimps, sweet sweet and sour sauce
- jasmine tea

* With 2 orders add one order of spare-ribs and one egg roll, free.

No. 3
Special for six People
- Three China Town soups
- Chicken with mushrooms
- Beef and pineapple
- Pork chow mein
- White rice, soy sauce
jasmine tea

With 2 orders and every subsequent order add two slices of roast pork

C

MENU

Burgers:
Plain hamburger
Plain cheeseburger
Double hamburger
Double cheeseburger

Sandwiches:
Hot dog
Ham & cheese
Tuna salad
Egg salad
Bacon, lettuce & tomato
Club sandwich

Side Orders:
Onion rings
French fries
Coleslaw
Lettuce & tomato salad

Fountain:
Banana split
Hot fudge sundae
Milk shake (chocolato,
vanilla or strawberry)

Beverages:
Coca Cola
Sprite
7-Up
Orange crush
Coffee
Milk

A. *Read the following advertisements for restaurants carefully.*

LING CHINESE RESTAURANT

Third Avenue at Buckson

Exotic Cantonese Food at reasonable prices

Reservations 426 2951

Also Take-away service

Open daily from 11 a.m. to 9 p.m.

ARLIE'S DELI

19 E. 33RD AT BELVIEW

- REAL KOSHER DILLS
- CHICKEN SOUP WITH MATZA BALLS
- HOMEMADE CORNED BEEF
- BLINTZES

OPEN 11 A.M. TO 11 P.M.

Gaylord's Restaurant

Good food at reasonable prices
Choice of three main dishes

Court Street and Maywood

Mon - Sat open 11 a.m. to 8 p.m.

BOB'S BURGER BARGAINS

Burgers   Shakes   Fries

Sundaes   Onion rings

1118 S. BROADWAY   OPEN 24 HOURS

Now decide which menu from the previous page (menu A, B, or C) belongs to these restaurants. There is one restaurant which does not have a menu. Write the letters in the place provided under the advertisements.

Oral Reinforcement

Compare your choices with the rest of the class and give reasons for your decisions.

B. *Refer to the menus and advertisements and choose the correct answers.*

1 You drink
  - (a) a banana split
  - (b) onion rings
  - (c) jasmine tea
  - (d) soy sauce

2 You eat
  - (a) orange crush
  - (b) milk
  - (c) sprite
  - (d) coleslaw

3 Which of the following do you use to add flavour to food?
  - (a) mustard
  - (b) sweet and sour sauce
  - (c) shark's fin soup
  - (d) two of the above

4 Which of these is not a dessert?
  - (a) hot fudge sundae
  - (b) peaches and cream
  - (c) blintzes
  - (d) kosher dills.

5 Which of these is not a main course?
  - (a) egg rolls
  - (b) veal cutlet with mashed potatoes
  - (c) spaghetti with meatballs
  - (d) pork chow mein

6 Which restaurant obviously does not serve 'take-away' food?
  - (a) Gaylord's
  - (b) Arlie's Deli
  - (c) Ling
  - (b) Bob's Burger

7 Which restaurant is open for the shortest period of time?
  - (a) Ling
  - (b) Bob's Burger
  - (c) Arlie's Deli
  - (d) Gaylord's

8 Which restaurant(s) do(es) not serve 'ethnic' food?
  - (a) Bob's Burger
  - (b) Gaylord's
  - (c) Ling
  - (d) Arlie's Deli

9 Which restaurant closes one day of the week?
  - (a) Bob's Burger
  - (b) Ling
  - (c) Arlie's Deli
  - (d) Gaylord's

10 In groups of three, put the restaurants in what you think would be the right order, from the least expensive to the most expensive.

least expensive. . . . .

. . . .

. . . .

most expensive. . . . .

. . . .

. . . .

Now compare your lists and discuss your decisions with the rest of the class.

TEXT 2

1 John Snoad is a young university student. He is working to pay for his education. He has very little money, but wants to invite his girlfriend Martha to have a meal with him.

2 Fred Harris is a businessman. He has very conservative taste in food but likes a large meal in the middle of the day. He wants to invite his secretary, Mrs Morris, to have a business lunch with him.

3 Peter and Susan Godfrey are a young couple with three small children. They like ethnic foods. Susan's rich parents are staying with them and they would like to have a restaurant dinner, but find it difficult to go out in the evening because of the children.

A. *Read the texts above and see if you can match the pictures to the descriptions of the people.*

B. *Look back at the menus given in Text 1 and decide which restaurant would be suitable for the different people described in Text 2. Discuss your decisions with the class.*

TEXT 3

Many people, male and female, like cooking. Actually most of the best cooks in the world are men.

Here are instructions on how to make English fruit and nut bars: (England is not famous for its fine food, but English sweets are amongst the best in the world!) Read the instructions carefully. Perhaps you can make these chocolate bars.

(a) First, go to your local supermarket and buy these things.

SHOPPING LIST

100 grams of plain chocolate
100 grams of butter
some sugar
175 grams of plain cookies
some almonds (about 50 grams)
some candied cherries

N.B. Plain chocolate is the very dark chocolate — not milk chocolate.
Plain cookies are not too sweet, but are not salty, either.

(b) Next go into your kitchen and find the following items.

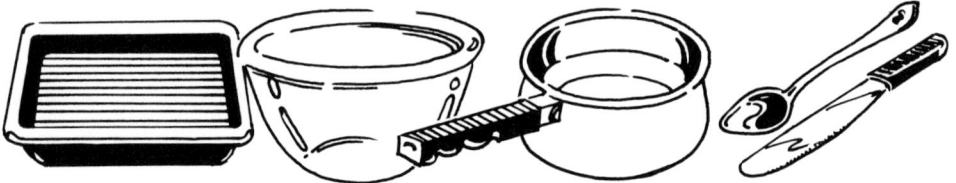

A shallow baking tin.   A pyrex bowl.   A saucepan.   A tablespoon   A knife.

N.B. A tablespoon is a big spoon!

(c) Now it is time to start cooking.

1 Put some water into a saucepan and put the saucepan on to the stove. Wait until the water is boiling.

2 Now put the chocolate, the butter and the sugar into the bowl, and set the bowl over the saucepan of boiling water. Wait until the chocolate, butter and sugar melt together, and then take the bowl out of the boiling water.

3 Break the cookies into very small pieces. Stir them into the chocolate mixture with a tablespoon.

60

4 Next, cut the almonds and the candied cherries into small pieces. Stir them into the mixture as well.

5 Grease the shallow baking tin with a little butter. Put the chocolate mixture into the greased baking tin and press it firmly down with the back of the tablespoon.

6 Put the baking tin into the refrigerator for two or three hours.

7 Finally, using a knife, cut the chocolate mixture into fruit and nut bars.

A. *According to the text you have just read, are the following statements true or false?*

1 In modern times women are much better cooks than men.	T	F
2 English sweets are not considered very good.	T	F
3 Fruit and nut bars are made with milk chocolate.	T	F
4 Approximately 50 grams of almonds are used in fruit and nut bars	T	F
5 A tablespoon is used for stirring coffee or tea.	T	F
6 The chocolate, butter and sugar are not put into the saucepan.	T	F
7 The almonds and the candied cherries are put into the chocolate mixture before the cookies.	T	F
8 Butter is put into the baking tin before the chocolate mixture.	T	F
9 The fruit and nut bars are baked in the oven.	T	F
10 The chocolate mixture is cut up into fruit and nut bars with a tablespoon.	T	F

B. *Arrange the following groups of letters to make words.*

1 ONOBLSEPAT

. . . .

2 IRUFT

. . . .

3 RISEHECR

. . . .

4 PCSNAAUE

. . . .

5 TLEM

. . . .

TEXT 1

WHALES

The whale is one of the few animals alive today which is similar to its prehistoric ancestors. This picture of a whale is on a rock wall in northern Norway. It is a Neolithic whale, drawn in approximately 2200 B.C.

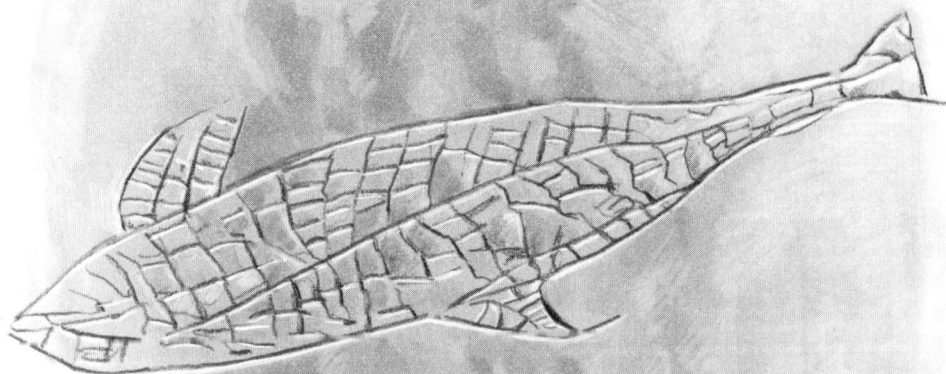

There are also pictures of whales on ancient Greek buildings, vases and coins. The wall paintings at the palace of Knossos in Crete are famous.

Most prehistoric animals were big. (The Blue Whale is the biggest animal living in the world today.)

62

For example, there are no mammoths alive today. They were too big. They failed to adapt to climatic changes, so now they are extinct.

Dinosaurs were also too big to survive on land, but they became aquatic. They went to live in the sea to support their massive body weight. Some scientists think that the whale is a direct descendant of the dinosaur.

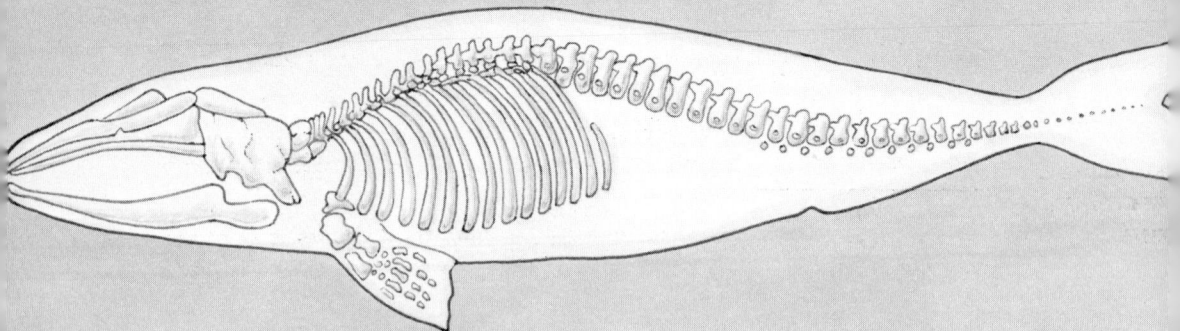

Look at this picture of the skeleton of a whale. Can you see the similarity between it and the shape of the dinosaur?

There are whales in all the oceans of the world. They make excursions to cold waters to find food. They swim to warmer waters to reproduce. They are mammals and they multiply by pairing, like all other types of mammals. The gestation period of a baby whale is one year.

Whales were in danger of extinction several years ago, but now they are protected by the laws of the International Convention for the Regulation of Whaling. However, whales are still hunted.

In Japan, they like eating whale-meat. In other places, the whale is used in the manufacture of margarine, detergents, cosmetics, vitamin pills, liver oil and insulin, among other products.

A. *Underline the correct statements.*

1 (a) The whale is a modern mammal which looks similar to its prehistoric ancestors.
   (b) Because the whale is a mammal it does not look similar to its prehistoric ancestors.

2 (a) Most prehistoric animals were big.
   (b) The whale is the biggest prehistoric animal alive today.

3 (a) Mammoths were too big to adapt to climatic conditions so they became extinct.
   (b) Dinosaurs went to live in the sea but were unable to adapt to aquatic conditions.

4 (a) Whales are mammals so they multiply by pairing.
   (b) After the pairing of adult whales, the baby whale is produced in cold waters.

5 (a) Whales were once in danger of extinction, but now they are never hunted.
   (b) Whales are now protected by law. However, they are still sometimes hunted.

B. *Find the answers to the following questions in the text.*

i   How do we know of the existence of whales in the world thousands of years ago?

    . . . .

    . . . .

ii What steps did the dinosaurs take in order to survive?

    . . . .

    . . . .

iii What do scientists assert, and why?

    . . . .

    . . . .

iv Why do whales sometimes prefer warm water and sometimes prefer cold water?

    . . . .

    . . . .

v   Why does man hunt the whale, and what arrangements are being made for its protection?

    . . . .

    . . . .

TEXT 2

There are two main types of whale — those which have teeth, and those which do not. One of the whales with teeth is the dolphin. Dolphins are fascinating creatures. There are many interesting stories about them. One of these stories is about a dolphin called Jack.

Jack lived in the sea off the shores of New Zealand. New Zealand is made up of two main islands. Between these, there is a stretch of sea called Cook Strait. Jack lived in Cook Strait.

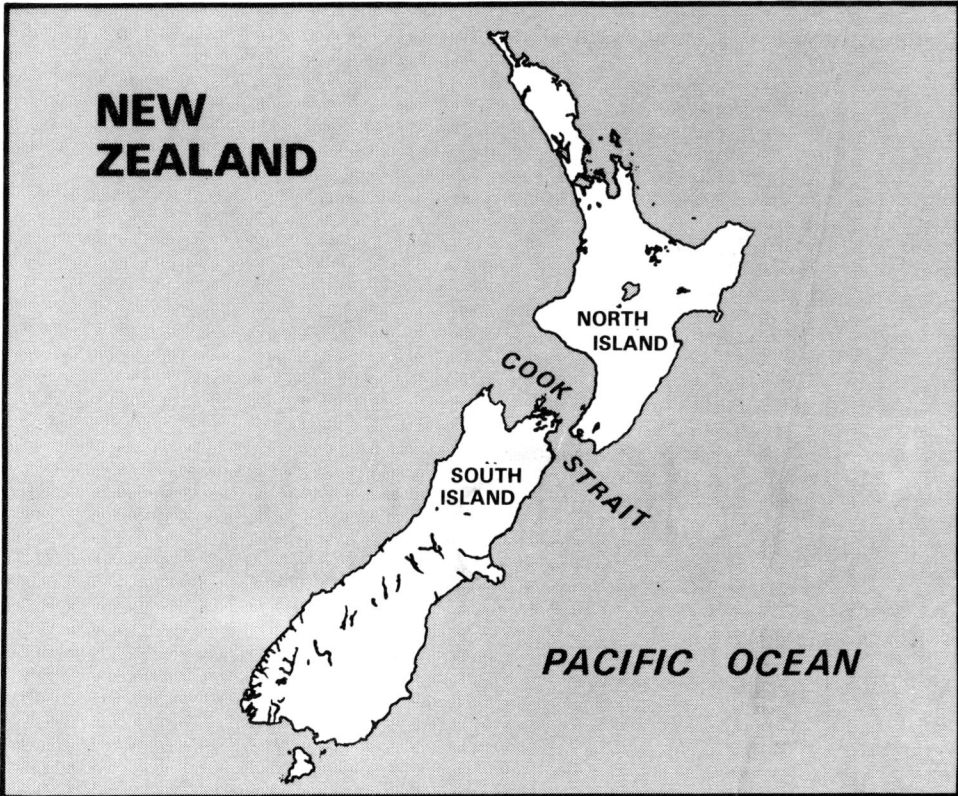

Jack first appeared in 1888. Jack used to swim in front of ships. Cook Strait is very difficult to navigate. It has very fast currents and a lot of rocks. Jack, the dolphin, led ships through this very dangerous strait. Sailors had tremendous faith in Jack. They felt he brought them luck. Everybody wanted to see this famous dolphin. Articles about Jack appeared in magazines and newspapers all over the world.

One day, Jack swam in front of a ship called the S.S. *Penguin*. One of the sailors was drunk. He shot Jack with his pistol. Immediately, the dolphin disappeared. Everybody was horrified!

Actually, Jack was not killed. A few days later, he appeared again and he continued to lead ships through Cook Strait for many years. But Jack never led the S.S. *Penguin* again. The S.S. *Penguin* became a bad luck ship, and sailors did not want to work on her. Eventually, the ship hit a rock and sank!

Jack was last seen in 1912. Perhaps he died of old age (he had been leading ships through Cook Strait for twenty-two years.) Perhaps he was killed. There were Norwegians hunting for whales in Cook Strait at the time. We can never know, but we do know this — Jack was one of the most famous dolphins ever.

A. *Complete the paragraph by filling it in with the appropriate words from the column on the right.*

The dolphin is one of various types of toothed . . . .   called

At the end of the nineteenth century and the beginning of the   ship

twentieth century, a very famous dolphin . . . . Jack   led

lived in Cook Strait. Cook Strait is a very . . . . stretch   shot

of water beteen the two main . . . . of New Zealand.   killed

    For many years, Jack . . . . ships safely through

Cook Strait! . . . . : wanted to see the famous dolphin.   disappeared

One day, a drunken sailor on the S.S. *Penguin* . . . .   whale

Jack. Fortunately, Jack was not . . . . , but he never   dangerous

led that . . . . through the Strait again. Jack finally   everybody

. . . . in 1912.   islands

B. *This is a conversation between a newspaper reporter and a sailor. Taking your information from Text 2, complete it.*

Reporter: I hear there's a famous dolphin that takes you through Cook Strait.

Sailor: . . . .

Reporter: Do you really think he leads you through the Strait to help the ship avoid difficulties?

Sailor: . . . .

Reporter: What makes Cook Strait so difficult to navigate?

Sailor: . . . .

Reporter: Why do you sailors dislike working on the S.S. *Penguin*?

Sailor:	. . . .
Reporter:	I hear that a drunken sailor fired a pistol at him. Is that true?
Sailor:	. . . .
Reporter:	Well, all this is very interesting! Thank you very much for answering my questions.

TEXT 3

1 It's the car of the century. The new General American Gazelle. It looks comfort-
2 able and it is. It looks fast and it is. It looks economical and it is: **32** ⁙⁙ **(23)** ⁙⁙
3 It always starts instantly, never fails to manoeuvre* smoothly.
4 All this is why they say that the Gazelle is the car of the century. See it soon at
5 your dealer's.

*To move easily in any direction.

A. *Match the words on the left with their definitions (according to the text) in the column on the right.*

(1)	(2)
century	to move easily
General American	the name of the car
Gazelle	a hundred years
economical	a car that doesn't use much gasoline
manoeuvre	a car showroom
dealer's	the name of the company

In the text:

1 century means. . . . .

2 . . . .

3 . . . .

4 . . . .

5 . . . .

6 . . . .

70

1 'It' in line 1 refers to . . . .

2 In line 2, the abbreviation for 'highway estimate' is

. . . .

3 The Gazelle gets 23 miles to the gallon of gasoline in the city; on the highway . . . .

4 In line 4, 'all this' refers to . . . .

5 In line 5, 'dealer's' is a short expression for . . . .

TEXT 1

The History of Thanksgiving Day

In the Autumn of 1621, the surviving Pilgrims (British settlers of Plymouth Colony in the State of Massachussetts, U.S.A.) numbered about a hundred. These brave settlers wished to give a feast in gratitude to God and to the Indians who showed them how to plant their crops, how to grow corn and to fertilize with dead fish. As a result of the Indians' help, the Pilgrims had a plentiful harvest which gave them sufficient food for the winter.

All of the Pilgrims and about seventy Indians attended the feast which lasted for four days. They drank no liquor, owing to their religious convictions, but they ate venison, wild turkey and squash, and a dish called succotash, made by the Indians from beans and corn.

They played games, had contests and smoked tobacco with the Indians. So, the tradition of a day of 'Thanksgiving' after the harvest (the fourth Thursday in November) was established by these courageous people.

A. *Read the following statements and circle* **YES** *or* **NO,** *as appropriate.*

1 The original residents of the United States were the British.	**YES**	**NO**
2 The Pilgrims were a religious group from Britain.	**YES**	**NO**
3 The native people of the region taught the Pilgrims how to plant their crops.	**YES**	**NO**
4 The Pilgrims and the Indians drank a lot of alcoholic drinks at the first Thanksgiving Feast.	**YES**	**NO**
5 Some of the food served at the first Thanksgiving Feast was Indian.	**YES**	**NO**

B. *Complete the paragraph by writing appropriate words in the blanks.*

Nowadays, people celebrate Thanksgiving . . . . a somewhat different way.

For university students, the Thanksgiving week-end . . . . the first long

holiday since the semester began in September. They usually try to . . . .

home to celebrate it with . . . . friends and relatives.

Thanksgiving Dinner typically consists . . . . a mandarin and olive salad

followed by a very large roast turkey stuffed . . . . giblet stuffing, cranberry

sauce, sweet potatoes, creamed potatoes, creamed onions and green beans. Most

people . . . . pumpkin pie for their Thanksgiving Day dessert, but mincemeat

pie . . . . also popular. Nearly everybody . . . . wine with the meal.

In the States, the Thanksgiving celebration is nearly as important . . . .

Christmas.

TEXT 2

Do you believe in Santa Claus or in Father Christmas? The surprising thing is that they are not the same person, but very few people remember that these days.

The original Santa Claus was St Nicholas. He was bishop of Myra, a town on the south coast of Turkey, during the fourth century. St Nicholas loved young children. There are several stories of how St Nicholas rescued children and young people from different dangerous situations. Dutch Protestants who went to live in New

Amsterdam (New York) took the legend of St Nicholas with them. In Dutch, he is called Sinter Class or San Klaas. North Americans loved the idea of the kind saint who gave children toys at Christmas-time. They renamed him Santa Claus.

Father Christmas is completely English. He first appeared in the Middle Ages in Christmas plays performed by the local working people. Father Christmas, as he was called, was initially modelled on Odin, the father of the Norse gods, who rode over the world on his eight-toed horse, Sleipnir, during the winter festivities, and checked that everybody was happy. Odin had a long beard and fur-trimmed cloak. The Father Christmas costume has really not changed very much from then to the present day.

Father Christmas did not bring English children toys until the days of Queen Victoria. In 1860, a picture of Father Christmas appeared on a Christmas card distributing presents to the children for the very first time. The idea was popular! Children loved it, of course. And so, Father Christmas started to bring toys on the night of 24 December for children to find when they woke up on the morning of 25 December, Christmas Day.

A. *Indicate whether (a) (b) (c) or (d) best completes the following sentences.*

1 A lot of people nowadays
  (a) remember that Santa Claus and Father Christmas are not the same person.
  (b) do not realize that Santa Claus and Father Christmas are the same person.
  (c) call Santa Claus by his original name, St Nicholas.
  (d) do not realize that Santa Claus and Father Christmas are not the same person.

2 St Nicholas
  (a) lived in Turkey sixteen hundred years ago.
  (b) used to dress up as Santa Claus, because he loved children.
  (c) was a great teacher who lived in Turkey in the fourth century.
  (d) went to live in New Amsterdam with the Dutch Protestants.

3 The name Santa Claus
  (a) was the name of the kind saint in Turkish.
  (b) was created by the North Americans, who took the Dutch name as a model.
  (c) is the name given to Old Father Christmas by the English.
  (d) is Dutch.

4 Father Christmas
  (a) was originally an English saint.
  (b) was originally a character in an English play in the Middle Ages.
  (c) is Odin, the father of the Norse gods.
  (d) rides Sleipnir, his eight-toed horse, on 24 December, when he take presents to all the children.

5 The first Father Christmas to distribute presents to children
  (a) was in the days immediately before Queen Victoria.
  (b) was in the U.S.A.
  (c) appeared on the morning of 25 December.
  (d) was on a Christmas card in 1860.

B. *Answer the following questions in complete sentences so that your answers make a short paragraph about Father Christmas.*

  (a) When and where did Father Christmas first appear?
  (b) Who was Father Christmas initially modelled on?
  (c) What did Odin look like and what clothes did he wear?
  (d) What appeared in 1860?
  (e) Who was the idea especially popular with?
  (f) So what did 'Father Christmas' start to bring English children?

  . . . .

  . . . .

  . . . .

  . . . .

  . . . .

  . . . .

  . . . .

  . . . .

TEXT 3

This is seventeen-year-old Patricia Hutchinson. She has made a Christingle. A Christingle is a table decoration which English people used to make at Christmas time. The custom has almost completely died out nowadays. Patricia was interviewed on television about her Christingle. This is a transcript of the interview.

Interviewer: Today, we have seventeen-year-old Patricia Hutchinson here in the studio with us. Hello, Patricia.

Patricia Hello!

Interviewer: Well, you have brought this Christingle to show us. I must say it is very pretty. Can you tell us something about it? Exactly what is a Christingle?

Patricia It's a table decoration. People used to make them a lot at Christmas-time.

Interviewer: What? Here in England?

Patricia Yes.

Interviewer: How long ago was that?

Patricia I don't really know, but they say people used to make them many years ago.

Interviewer: How are Christingles made?

Patricia Well, basically, it's a large orange. You cut off a piece of orange-peel from the bottom of the orange.

Interviewer: Why do you do that?

Patricia So that it stands firmly and doesn't fall over.

Interviewer: I see!

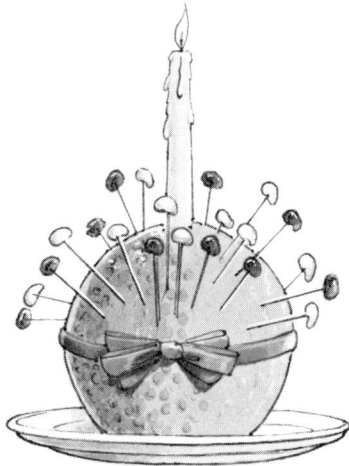

Patricia	Then, you cut a hole in the top of the orange and put a coloured candle into it.
Interviewer:	Yes!
Patricia	Then, you just put peanuts and raisins on to the ends of some cocktail sticks and put the other ends into the orange.
Interviewer:	And, finally, you tie some red ribbon round the orange.
Patricia	Yes. People say the candle represents Christ, the light of the world. The nuts and the fruit are the fruits of the earth. The orange represents the world and the red ribbon symbolizes the blood of Christ.
Interviewer:	Well, this is all very interesting. Patricia has certainly shown us a very unusual table decoration, hasn't she? Thank you very much, Patricia.

A. *Are the following statements true or false?*

1 Patricia Hutchinson has made a table decoration.	T	F
2 Many people make Christingles in England nowadays.	T	F
3 Christingles are decorated with raisins but not with peanuts.	T	F
4 The orange represents the fruits of the earth.	T	F
5 The blood of Christ is represented by a red ribbon round the Christingle	T	F

B. *Complete the following paragraph by putting the missing verbs into the appropriate form.*

Patricia Hutchinson is in the television studio because she . . . . (make) a

Christingle. Many years ago in England, people . . . . (use) to make

Christingles every Christmas. People . . . . (say) that the peanuts and raisins

represent the fruits of the earth, while the orange itself . . . . (symbolize) the

world. Patricia . . . . (show) the viewers the Christingle she had made.

TEXT 1

Henry VIII

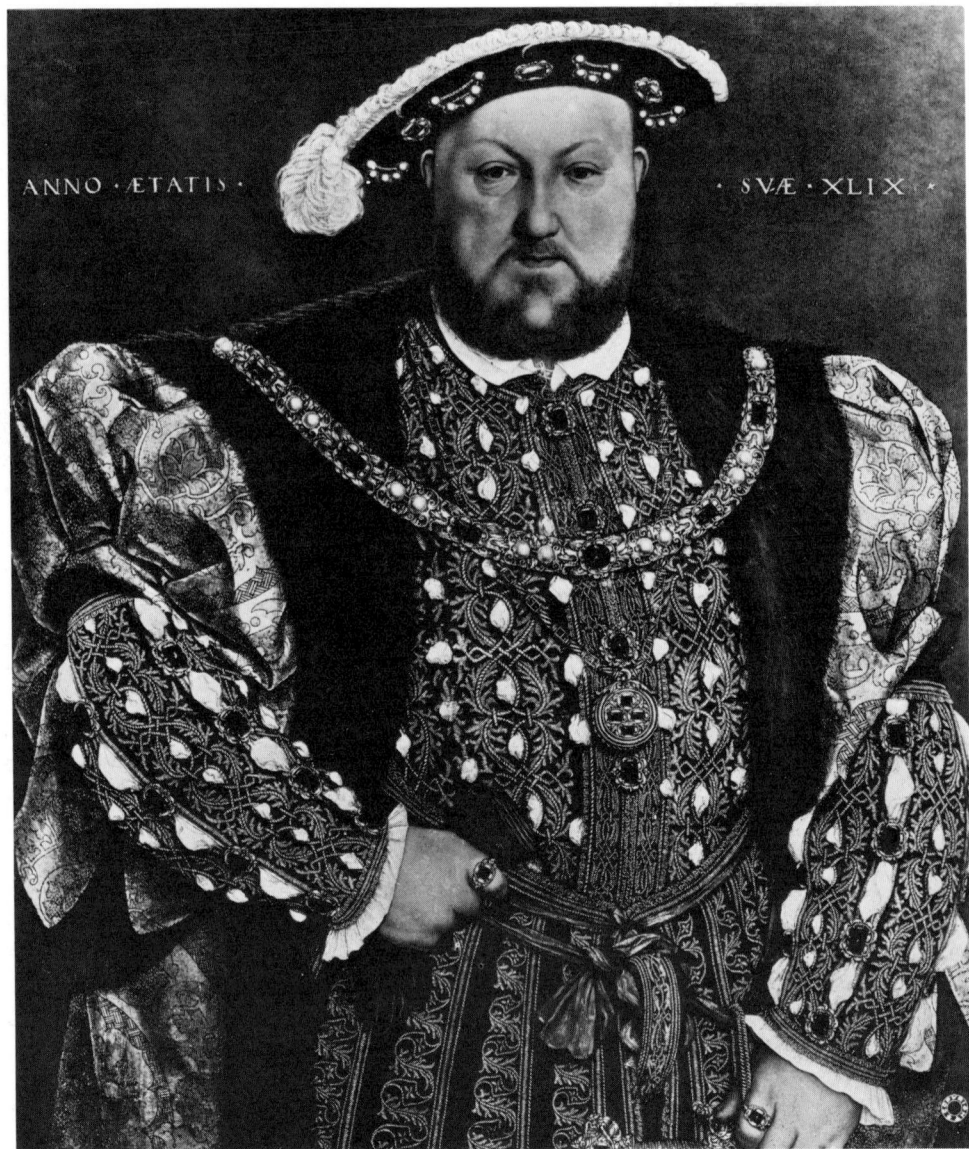

ANNO · ÆTATIS ·   SVÆ · XLIX ·

Catherine of Aragon

Ann Boleyn

Jane Seymour

Ann of Cleves

Catherine Howard

Catherine Parr

Henry VIII was born in 1491. He was the second son of Henry VII and Elizabeth of York. He had an elder brother called Arthur. Arthur married Catherine of Aragon. Henry was handsome and athletic. He was intelligent and loved music. In 1502, his brother Arthur died, so, when Henry VII died in 1509, Henry became King of England. He married Catherine of Aragon, his brother's widow, in the same year.

Henry and Catherine had no male children (no future king), so they divorced. This alienated the Pope, and Henry VIII was excommunicated. Henry then became Supreme Head of the new Protestant Church of England. This is still the official religion in England today.

In 1533, Henry married Anne Boleyn, who was one of Catherine's ladies-in-waiting. They had one daughter (later the very famous Elizabeth I) but no sons, so Henry was still not satisfied. He had Anne executed in 1536 and married Jane Seymour, who was one of Anne's ladies-in-waiting! Jane had a son, the future Edward VI, but unfortunately she died almost immediately.

Henry married Anne of Cleves in 1540, but then he did not think she was sufficiently beautiful, so he divorced her a few weeks after the wedding ceremony. Next, he married Catherine Howard, but he had to execute her for infidelity in 1542.

Henry's sixth wife was Catherine Parr. She was his final wife! Henry VIII, King of England, died in 1547.

A. Are the following statements **RIGHT** or **WRONG?** Circle as appropriate.

1 Henry was not the only son of Henry VII and Elizabeth of York.　　**RIGHT**　　**WRONG**

2 Catherine of Aragon married three times.　　**RIGHT**　　**WRONG**

3 Henry and Catherine divorced because they had different ideas on religion.　　**RIGHT**　　**WRONG**

4 Henry VIII was excommunicated because he divorced Anne Boleyn.　　**RIGHT**　　**WRONG**

5 Anne Boleyn died in her bed.　　**RIGHT**　　**WRONG**

6 Anne Boleyn and Jane Seymour did similar work before they married Henry.　　**RIGHT**　　**WRONG**

7 Queen Jane's son Edward died almost immediately after he was born.　　**RIGHT**　　**WRONG**

8 Anne of Cleves was a very attractive girl.　　**RIGHT**　　**WRONG**

9 Henry VIII divorced Catherine Howard because of her infidelity.　　**RIGHT**　　**WRONG**

10 Henry VIII was not married when he died.　　**RIGHT**　　**WRONG**

B. Using the text as your guide, fill in the missing information from the following sentences on the life of Henry VIII.

1 Henry was born in the year

2 He became King of England at the age of

3 Henry married　　　　　　　times.

4 Henry's first wife was Catherine of Aragon. It was her　　　　　　　marriage.

5 Anne Boleyn was the Queen of England for only　　　　　　　years.

6 Queen Jane, Henry's third wife, died shortly after the birth of her son,

7 The King divorced　　　　　　　, because he thought she was ugly.

8 Catherine Howard, Henry's　　　　　　　wife, was executed in 1542.

9 The last lady Henry married was

10 Henry VIII died in 1547 at the age of

TEXT 2

The Tower is one of the most famous monuments in London. In the past, it has been a castle of residence and a prison. Both Anne Boleyn and Catherine Howard were executed there. Nowadays, it is a famous museum. The Crown Jewels are probably its greatest attraction. These are so valuable that the police guard them day and night.

It is not always possible to see the Crown Jewels. Visitors should first study the following information about admission, before going along to the Tower.

ADMISSION TO VIEW THE CROWN JEWELS
FROM 1 MARCH TO 31 OCTOBER

Weekdays open 9.30 am   *Sundays* open 2 pm
Last ticket sold for admission to:
    Tower of London   5 pm   Tower of London   5 pm
    Jewel House   5.45 pm   Jewel House   5.30 pm
FROM 1 NOVEMBER TO 28 FEBRUARY
Weekdays only open 9.30 am   (not open Sundays)
Last ticket sold for admission to:
    Tower of London   4 pm
    Jewel House   4.30 pm
Closed Christmas Day and Good Friday

SEASON TICKETS, valid for a year from the date of issue, admit their holders to all ancient monuments and historic buildings in the care of the State. Tickets can be purchased at many monuments; at HMSO bookshops; and from the Department of the Environment (AMHB/P), 25 Savile Row, London W1X 2BT, who will supply full information on request.

A. *Answer the following questions briefly.*

1 Is the Tower of London always open on Sundays?

. . . .

2 Can visitors see the Crown Jewels at 5 p.m. on weekdays during the summer?

. . . .

3 On which days during the winter is it impossible to see the fabulous Crown Jewels?

. . . .

4 Is it absolutely necessary to go to the Tower in order to buy tickets to see the Crown Jewels?

. . . .

5 Where else can an admission ticket be brought?

. . . .

B. *Selecting from the column of prepositions on the right, complete the following passage.*

Tickets for admission .....to.... the Jewel House can be

bought either in the Tower of London or ....at.. HMSO

bookshops. They can also be obtained ....at... the

Department of the Environment. ....On.... request, the

Department of the Environment will also supply visitors

...with.. complete information ..about.. the Crown

Jewels and the Tower of London. You can purchase a season

ticket to all Britain's state monuments. This ticket is valid

....for... a year ...from.. the date you acquired it.

Remember, the Tower of London is closed on Sundays

.bet.... the beginning of November and the end of

February. People from all ..over.... the world go to the

Tower of London especially to see this amazing collection of

jewels.

for
at
from
about
to
between
with
over
on
after

TEXT 3

The toy of the century

Ernö Rubik comes from Hungary. He is an architect and designer. He wanted to help his students to understand three-dimensional problems, so he invented the Rubik Cube.

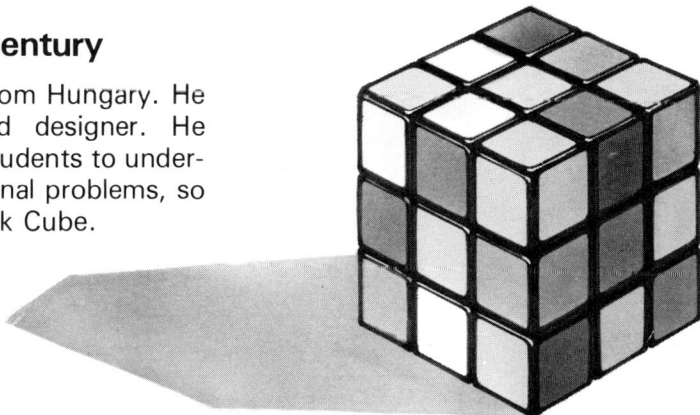

The cube is made of twenty-six movable pieces. These pieces are coloured. They are usually green, blue, red, orange, yellow and white. The idea is that you must twist the sections of the cube until all the green pieces are together on one side, all the blue pieces together on another side, etc.

The cube is tremendously popular nearly everywhere in the world. Rubik cubes have become one of Hungary's most important exports. People say the cube is 'the toy of the century'. Cubes are certainly good value for money, because normally everybody in the family likes to play with them. People want to see how long it takes them to solve the cube. There are cube competitions everywhere. The best cube-masters can solve the problem in under thirty seconds! However, solving the Rubik Cube is difficult for most people, so several experts have written books to show us how to solve the cube.

A. *Match the phrases in Column **A** with those in Column **B** to make correct sentences.*

A	B
1 Ernö Rubik is the man	to help his students.
2 He invented the cube	the whole family likes to play with it.
3 Rubik's students could not solve three-dimensional problems	a very important industry in Hungary.
4 The cube is good value for money because	who designed the Rubik Cube.
5 The manufacture of the Rubik Cube is	so Rubik made the cube to help them.

1 ....

2 ....

3 ....

4 ....

5 ....

B. *Arrange the following groups of words into correct sentences. The five re-arranged sentences make a short paragraph about Rubik and the Rubik Cube.*

Rubik Hungarian architect designer and is a. He his students

. . . .

wanted three-dimensional problems to understand. He his cube famous

. . . .

designed and made. Now to play everybody wants Rubik Cube with the.

. . . .

The Hungary's most important exports cube one of is.

. . . .